THᴇ
WHISTLING

by Duncan Abel and
Rachel Wagstaff

Based on the novel by
Rebecca Netley

ISBN 978-0-573-00070-6

concordtheatricals.co.uk
concordtheatricals.com

FOR AMATEUR PRODUCTION ENQUIRIES

UNITED KINGDOM AND WORLD
EXCLUDING NORTH AMERICA
licensing@concordtheatricals.co.uk
020-7054-7298

Each title is subject to availability from Concord Theatricals, depending upon country of performance.

This work is published by Samuel French, an imprint of Concord Theatricals Ltd.

The Professional Rights in this play are controlled by United Agents Ltd, 12-26 Lexington St, London W1F 0LE.

USE OF COPYRIGHTED MUSIC

USE OF COPYRIGHTED THIRD-PARTY MATERIALS

IMPORTANT BILLING AND CREDIT REQUIREMENTS

NOTE

This edition reflects a rehearsal draft of the script and may differ from the final production.

THE WHISTLING was originally produced by The Mill at Sonning Theatre, and premiered there on 27th September 2024. The cast and creative team were as follows:

GREER . . . . Raghad Chaar

MISS GILLIES . . . . Stephanie Farrell

ELSPETH . . . . Rebecca Forsyth

AILSA . . . . Heather Jackson

HETTIE . . . . Nadia Kramer

PATERSON / DOCTOR / ROBERT ARGYLE . . . . Jonny McGarrity

BRIDGET . . . . Susie Riddell

MARY . . . . Sophie Bidgood, Ivy Evans, Saffron Haynes

Writers . . . . Duncan Abel and Rachel Wagstaff

Director/Joint Movement Director . . . . Joseph Pitcher

Joint Movement Director . . . . Alex Christian

Set Designer . . . . Diego Pitarch

Costume Designer . . . . Natalie Titchener

Composer & Sound Designer . . . . Simon Arrowsmith

Lighting Designer . . . . Richard J. Jones

Illusionist . . . . Guy Barrett

Casting . . . . Pearson Casting CDG CDA CSA

Children's Casting . . . . Amber Edlin

THE MILL

SONNING

Set majestically on the banks of the River Thames, the historic Mill at Sonning Theatre first opened as a theatre in 1982, and has garnered decades of entertainment excellence as one of the UK's only dinner theatres. It won the UK Theatre Award for Best Musical Production (*Gypsy*, 2023) and also won the UK Theatre Award for most welcoming theatre three years in a row (2016, 2017, 2018).

The Mill, a full production house, builds sets and designs costumes on-site, offering plays, musicals, concerts, magic, comedy nights, and special events year-round. Tickets include a freshly prepared two-course meal in a riverside restaurant, and a seat in an intimate, air-conditioned 217-capacity theatre. A Riverside Bar, with the original waterwheel still in operation, serves Afternoon Tea with outdoor terrace seating.

In 2005, the venue launched the first Hydro Electric Scheme to be powered by the natural resources of the River Thames. The sustainable scheme generates enough electric energy for the theatre's numerous lights – arc lights, spotlights, footlights, house lights – but also for the restaurant dining rooms, bars, ovens, as well as backstage corridors, dressing rooms, wardrobe areas, set construction workshops and control box, in addition to its many, many offices.

The theatre is a family-run business. The founders were Tim and Eileen Richards. Their daughter Sally Hughes is the managing director and Sally's son, Adam Rolston, became co-managing director in 2023.

CAST

RAGHAD CHAAR | Greer

Raghad is an alumna of The Royal Conservatoire of Scotland where she trained in BA Acting.

Theatre Credits: *Mary, The Last Farewell* (Edinburgh Festival); *How to Hold Your Breath* (Royal Court); *Two Ladies* (Bridge Theatre, Dir Sir Nicholas Hytner); *Revolutions Days* (A One Woman Show at The Roxy, Edinburgh and Tramway, Glasgow).

TV Credits: *The State* (Channel 4, Dir Peter Kosminsky); *Collateral* (Netflix, Dir S.J.Clarkson); *I Hate Suzie* (Sky Atlantic, Dir Georgi Banks-Davies).

Film Credits: *Star Wars: Episode IX – The Rise of Skywalker* (Disney, Dir J.J. Abrams); *Ignacio De Loyola* (Dir Paolo Dy) and various short films including *Adnan* and *Fireworks*.

Voice Credits: *Gaming: Hood: Outlaws & Legends*, *Diablo IV*, and *Total War Pharaoh*.

Audio Credits: *Arabian Nights Volume 1 & 2*, *The Sandman*, *Sleeping Beauty*, *Rani Takes on the World: Beyond Bannerman Road* and various other audiobooks and plays.

Raghad is a winner of the AudioFile Earphones Award.

STEPHANIE FARRELL | Miss Gillies

Stephanie trained at ArtsEd where she received her BA in Acting. Theatre credits include *Witchcraft* (Finborough Theatre); *Knives in Hens* (The King's Head); *Killing Alan* (Underbelly Theatre); *Book the Babysitter* (Soho Theatre).

TV credits include the upcoming *Lockerbie* (Sky Arts) starring Colin Firth.

Writing includes *Bleed Between the Lines* (an Inner Seasons Poetry collection) and *Kaleidoscopic Minds*: An anthology of poetry by neurodivergent women co-edited by Stephanie in association with The Autistic Girls Network. Her writing has featured in several anthologies and publications and she has hosted poetry events at The Southbank Centre and Henley Literary Festival.

Stephanie narrates Alexander McCall Smith's *Isabel Dalhousie* audiobook series, as well as voicing multiple TV and Radio campaigns and animations include Disney Pixar's *Brave*.

REBECCA FORSYTH | Elspeth

Earlier this year Rebecca played co-lead Gisela Schertling at the Traverse Theatre, Edinburgh, in new play *Storm Lantern* (Strange Town Touring Company), having been part of the original touring cast in 2022. She has toured extensively with *Antigone na h'Éireann*, *Women of the Mourning Fields* (Aulos Productions); *The Shakespeares*, *Scenes From A Marriage* (Storyboard Theatre) and *Balisong* (Strange Town Touring Company/ Fast Forward Productions). Other theatre credits include *Trojan Barbie* (New Celts Productions), *Twelfth Night, Men Should Weep* and *The Three Sisters* (Edinburgh Napier University). Screen credits include *The Crown* (Left Bank/Sony/Netflix), *Butterfly* (BFI/Screen Education Edinburgh), *Leekdown* (Media Education) and *The Mouse* (Screen Academy Scotland).

HEATHER JACKSON | Ailsa

Heather was born in Falkirk, Scotland. She studied Drama at Queen Margaret University in Edinburgh and voice with Jeanette Mackay. She has enjoyed a varied career and was delighted to play the role of Madame Giry in the West End production of *The Phantom of the Opera* for a total of nine years, leaving the show in 2009.

Other theatre credits include: Mother Lord in *High Society* (The Mill, Sonning); Ambassador in *Roman Holiday* (Theatre Royal, Bath); Mrs Higgins in *My Fair Lady* (UK Tour and London Coliseum); Andy in *Stepping Out* (Perth Rep); Principal Soloist in *Broadway Dusseldorf* created by Arlene Phillips (Capitol Theater, Dusseldorf); *My Fair Lady* (directed by Simon Callow, National Tour); *Pirates of Penzance* (National Tour); Principal Soloist in *The West End Revue* (Talk of London); Prince Charming in *Cinderella* (Borderline Theatre Company); Princess in *Aladdin* and *Jack and the Beanstalk* (MacRobert Arts Centre); Fiona McScratchit in *Mr McScrooge* (Glasgow Pavilion) and Jesse and Virginia in *Beckett's Last Act* (Tour).

Heather spent five happy years in The Stadium Theatre Company working onboard the P&O cruise ships Canberra, Oriana and Victoria, performing roles as diverse as Ado Annie in *Oklahoma*, Madame Dubonet in *The Boyfriend*, Vi Petty in *Buddy* and Eliza in *My Fair Lady*. She also headlined in her own solo classical concerts.

On TV Heather played Catherine Galbraith in *Take the High Road* and was the face of *Woman* and *Woman's Own* magazines in a major advertising campaign. She was a guest artist on *The Judy Spiers Show* on Radio 2. Film credits include: *Rise of the Beast, The Area 51 Incident, Tooth Fairy 2* and *Candy Witch*.

NADIA KRAMER | Hettie

Nadia trained in musical theatre at the MGA Academy of Performing Arts in Edinburgh. Her theatre credits include Sophie Sheridan in *Mamma Mia!* (Royal Caribbean/Littlestar Productions) and Stephanie Mangano in *Saturday Night Fever The Musical* (Royal Caribbean), Tigerlily in *Peter Pan* (Royal and Derngate Northampton, Crossroads Pantomimes) and Princess Jasmine in *Aladdin* (The Albert Halls, Polka Dot Pantomimes).

Nadia is very excited to be part of such a spine chilling piece of theatre at The Mill at Sonning.

JONNY MCGARRITY | Paterson/Doctor/Robert

Jonny trained at The Arts Educational Schools (ArtsEd) London, almost 20 years after studying Law at Newcastle University.

Theatre credits: *A Little Princess* (Theatre By The Lake); *The Full Monty* (UK No.1 Tour); *The Girl on the Train* (English Theatre Frankfurt); *Fucking Men* (King's Head Theatre); *The Censor* (Hope Theatre); *Shakespeare and Jersey – Secrets Unlocked* (Butterfly Theatre Company); *The Taming of the Shrew* (Tristan Bates Theatre); *The Peregrine* (Stockwell Playhouse); *The Merchant of Venice* (Cockpit Theatre); *A Midsummer Night's Dream* (Butterfly Theatre Company); *An Ideal Husband*, (Butterfly Theatre Company); *Swing By Around 8* (Ghostlight Theatre).

Musical Theatre credits: *A Christmas Carol* (Folkoperan, Stockholm).

Screen credits: *A Scottish Love Scheme* (Hallmark / White Stag / Studio BRB); *Coronation Street* (Granada/ITV); *Without Guilt* (Wiedemann & Berg TV); *Emmerdale* (ITV); *Outlander* (Left Bank Pictures).

SUSIE RIDDELL | Bridget

Susie trained at the Royal Welsh College of Music & Drama, and the ITV Junior Workshop.

Theatre includes: *Other Desert Cities* (The Old Vic); *Transmissions* (Birmingham Rep); *What if the Plane Falls Out of the Sky* (Idiot Child/ Bristol Old Vic); *You're Not Doing It Right* (Idiot Child/Tobacco Factory); *Nostalgia* (Theatre West); *The Brummie Patrocleia* (Arcola); *Macbeth*, *The Tempest*, *The Taming of the Shrew* and *Twelfth Night* (Oddsocks Productions); *The Bad One* (Women & Theatre); *Three Sisters* (RWCMD)

TV includes: *Grace IV*, *Coronation Street* and *Emmerdale* (ITV); *Doctors*, *Gavin & Stacey*, *Saxondale* (BBC), *Combat Trains* (Woodcut Media/ History Channel)

Film includes: *The People Before* (Sea High Productions); *An Idiot's Guide to Being Thirty* (BBC Studios)

Radio/Audio: As a member of the BBC Radio Drama Company, Susie has appeared in a great many radio dramas including *Ulysses*, *The Great Gatsby*, *Mrs Dalloway*, *1984*, *Tamburlaine*, *Frankenstein*, *The Little Ottleys*, *A Farewell to Arms*, *Home Front*, *Shardlake: Dark Fire*, *The History of Titus Groan* and *A Charles Paris Mystery: An Amateur Corpse* (BBC Radio 4 & 3); *D-Day at 70*, *The Battle of Britain at 75* (BBC Radio 2/TBI Media); *VE Day at 70* (Classic FM/TBI Media); *Blakes 7: Ministry of Truth* and *Doom's Day: Dawn of an Everlasting Peace* (Big Finish).

Susie plays Tracy Horrobin in BBC Radio 4's *The Archers*. She has narrated over 60 audiobooks, and co-produces the podcast *Limited Time Only*.

SOPHIE BIDGOOD | Mary

Sophie is twelve years old and comes from Wokingham. She has attended Steppin Out Theatre School for seven years. Sophie is delighted to be returning to The Mill at Sonning having made her professional debut last year playing Baby Louise in *Gypsy*. In her spare time Sophie loves reading, anything to do with Harry Potter and making miniature props!! She would like to thank her family and friends for their continued support. Sophie is represented by EJC Management.

IVY EVANS | Mary

Ivy is a local performer and has recently played the title role in the musical *Annie* for her local theatre group. Ivy is a keen voice artist, you can also hear her playing characters on many animated series streaming on Netflix.

Ivy is delighted to be making her professional stage debut in *The Whistling* at The Mill.

In her spare time Ivy loves to dance, sing, swim and spend time with her family and friends.

SAFFRON HAYNES | Mary

Saffron trains with Sylvia Young Saturday School and Spirit Musical Theatre Classes.

Professional Credits Include: Educational Video for Tate Britain.

The role of Mary marks Saffron's theatrical debut, and she is thrilled to embark on this exciting journey.

Outside of her acting pursuits, Saffron enjoys reading, roller skating, and taking care of her two mischievous sausage dogs, Snoopy and Ziggy. She is represented by PD Management and is looking forward to the opportunities that lie ahead in her blossoming career.

CREATIVE

DUNCAN ABEL | Writer

Duncan's original new play, *Room 13*, opens at The Barn Theatre in Autumn 2024 (co-written with Rachel Wagstaff). Also with Wagstaff, Duncan has co-written the multi-award-winning adaptations of *The Da Vinci Code* (UK Tour, Ogunquit Playhouse) and *The Girl on the Train* (UK Tour/Duke of York's). Duncan has also written for BBC Radio 4 and Sing London.

His short stories are published in various literary anthologies. He is currently under commission to several UK theatre companies.

RACHEL WAGSTAFF | Writer

Rachel wrote the book for *Flowers for Mrs Harris*, which transferred to Chichester Festival Theatre after premiering at the Sheffield Crucible. The original production won the UK Theatre Award for Best Musical and the London premiere at Riverside Studios won the WhatsOnStage Award for Best Off West End Production. For Agatha Christie Ltd she adapted *The Mirror Crack'd*, which toured the UK with the Wales Millenium Centre and Wiltshire Creative, and recently toured the UK in a new production by Original Theatre.

Her award-winning adaptation of Sebastian Faulks' *Birdsong* is currently on its fifth UK Tour, having opened in the West End. Rachel's musical *Moonshadow*, co-written with Yusuf Islam (Cat Stevens) was previewed at the Royal Albert Hall and performed at the Princess Theatre in Melbourne. She also wrote the book for the original musical *Only The Brave*, which opened at the Wales Millennium Centre. With Duncan Abel, Rachel adapted Dan Brown's *The Da Vinci Code*, which toured the UK and made its multi-award-winning US premiere at the Ogunquit Playhouse; and Paula Hawkins' *The Girl on the Train*, which had a record-breaking UK tour and West End run and is now performed across the UK and beyond, with a new tour opening in January 2025. Also co-written with Duncan Abel, *Room 13* opens at The Barn in Cirencester in Autumn 2024.

Rachel adapted Sebastian Faulks' novel *The Girl at the Lion d'Or* as a five-part series and, with Duncan Abel, wrote *When I Lost You*, both for Radio 4.

She has multiple TV and feature film adaptations in development.

REBECCA NETLEY | Author, Original Novel

Rebecca Netley grew up as part of an eccentric family in a house full of books and music, and these things have fed her passions. Family and writing remain at the heart of Rebecca's life; she lives in Reading with her family and an overenthusiastic dog, who gives her writing tips.

Rebecca is a writer of long and short fiction; her debut novel, *The Whistling* (Penguin, 2021), won the Exeter Novel Prize and was longlisted for the Michael Ondaatje Prize. *The Whistling* has been adapted for stage. It was followed by *The Black Feathers* which was published by Michael Joseph in 2023.

JOSEPH PITCHER | Director/Joint Movement Director

Joseph's directing credits include *Gypsy* (Mill at Sonning, Winner of the UK Theatre Award for Best Musical Production 2023); *Macbeth* (Salomons, Tunbridge Wells); *The Producers* (Theatre on the Bay, Cape Town, Winner of the Fleur Du Cap Award for Best Production 2021); *Kipps* (Arts Educational Schools); *High Society*, *Singin' in the Rain*, *Guys & Dolls*, *My Fair Lady* (all Mill at Sonning) and *Snoopy The Musical* (Jermyn Street Theatre).

Joseph is Associate Director of the RSC's production of *Matilda The Musical*, which he has directed in Japan, South Africa, Israel and Holland. He was Resident Director on *Matilda* in London's West End for two years.

As an actor, he appeared in *The Winter's Tale* (RSC); *Anything Goes* (Royal National Theatre/Theatre Royal, Drury Lane); *Singin' in the Rain* (Royal National Theatre/West Yorkshire Playhouse); *Dangerous Corner* (New Vic, Stoke); *A Midsummer Night's Dream*, *Macbeth*, *Lady Be Good*, *The Boyfriend* (all Regent's Park Open Air Theatre); *Oklahoma!* (National tour); *Fallen in Love* (Red Rose Chain); *The Lion, the Witch and the Wardrobe* (West Yorkshire Playhouse/Birmingham Rep); *Alice in Wonderland* (Birmingham Rep); *Sisterly Feelings* (Bristol Old Vic); *Love's A Luxury* (The Mill at Sonning); *Chicago* (Adelphi Theatre); *Sunset Boulevard* (National tour); *Me and My Girl* (National Tour) and *The Boyfriend* (National tour).

Joseph and his brother run TextileArtist.org, an online subscription-based business providing workshops in textile and mixed media art techniques. He co-invented the board game Game for Fame, which topped Amazon's Best Selling Board Game list for three years running.

ALEX CHRISTIAN | Joint Movement Director

Alex's performing and creative work includes West End, Regional & International Productions and TV & Film. Most recently he has been Resident Choreographer on shows such as Disney's *Newsies* and *The Phantom of the Opera*, and Associate Choreographer on *Gypsy* at The Mill at Sonning which won the UK Theatre Award for Best Musical. Some of his other credits include: Choreographer on *Celebrating Sondheim Concert* (Chichester Festival Theatre); *Love Never Dies Concert* (Theatre Royal Drury Lane), Baby John in *West Side Story* (Leicester Curve), Dance Captain on *Oklahoma!* (Chichester Festival Theatre), Doody in *Grease* (UK Tour), Dance Captain on *Flashdance* (UK & International Tour), Dance Captain on *Guys & Dolls* (The Mill at Sonning), *She Loves Me* (Sheffield Crucible), *Kiss Me Kate* (UK Tour). He has also featured as a dancer in Disney's movies *Snow White* and *Disenchanted*.

DIEGO PITARCH | Set Designer

Diego Pitarch was born in Valencia, Spain, where he trained as an architect.

In 1992 he moved to Paris, France, to complete a four year course in Interior Design at the prestigious E.S.A.G. School of Design. For his final diploma he was declared first of his promotion and obtained an excellency award for his thesis in Theatre Design.

While in Paris he collaborated with the prestigious American designer Hilton McConnico. Amongst other projects Diego contributed to the design of an exhibition celebrating the "Carre" Hermes at the Suntory Museum in Osaka, Japan.

1999 saw Diego relocating to London to study at the Slade School of Art where he successfully completed his MA in Theatre Design. In 2001 he was selected for the Linbury Prize and his design – for Katya Kabanova for the Welsh National Opera – placed him amongst the finalists.

Since then Diego has developed a career as an International Theatre Designer, collaborating with renowned directors and companies. His work has appeared in theatres across the UK, Europe and the Caribbean. Some of his recent successes include *Sunset Boulevard* in London's West End; *Spend, Spend, Spend*, which won a TMA award for Best Musical in 2009; the 2011 European tour of *The Who's Tommy*; the 2013 UK and Ireland tour of *Fiddler on the Roof* starring Paul Michael Glaser and the 2014 UK touring production of *Fame*.

NATALIE TITCHENER | Costume Designer

Natalie trained in Fashion Design, Jewellery Design and Print Making before studying a degree in Costume Design at the Wimbledon School of Art.

Natalie has spent many years working in Wardrobe and Costume Production. Experience includes Disney, The National Theatre, The Royal Opera House and Eton College.

Productions include: *Hercules, Disney Dreams* (Disney); *Humble Boy, South Pacific, The Loft Season* (The National Theatre); *Madam Butterfly, The Magic Flute, La Traviata, Tosca, Tales of Hoffman, Wozzeck, Turandot* (The Royal Opera House); *A Winter's Tale, Twelfth Night, The White Devil, Death of a Salesman, Pravada, The Lady Killers, The Government Inspector, Oh What a Lovely War* (Eton College); *Blithe Spirit, The Hollow, High Society, Dead Simple, Improbable Fiction, Spider's Web, My Fair Lady, The Unexpected Guest, Ten Times Table, Gaslight, Guys & Dolls, Private Lives, Towards Zero, Singin' in the Rain, Top Hat, Gypsy, High Society, Twelfth Night, Bedroom Farce* (The Mill at Sonning Theatre).

SIMON ARROWSMITH | Composer & Sound Designer

Simon has always been fascinated by telling stories with sound. He graduated from Manchester Metropolitan University with a Bachelor's and Master's in Contemporary Arts. His theatre work has been selected for festivals and showcases including London's ICA, Manchester's Greenroom and as part of the National Review of Live Art.

Music composition and sound design work includes: *Help! We Are Still Alive* (Seven Dials Playhouse); *Macbeth* (The Shakespeare Project); *The Lesson, The House of Yes* (The Hope Theatre); *Thrill Me* (Jermyn Street Theatre); *Checkpoint Chana* (The Finborough); *The View from Nowhere* (Park Theatre); *Something Something Lazarus* (King's Head); *April in Paris* (English Theatre of Hamburg); *Two Gentlemen of Verona, Jekyll & Hyde* (White Horse Theatre, Germany) and *The Collectors of Screams* (The Pleasance). He has been nominated for multiple Off-West End ('Offie') awards for his sound designs and is a joint winner of a Standing Ovation Award for Best Theatricality. As well as his work in theatre he composes music for films and games.

When he's not writing music, he works as a story consultant, helping people and organisations to find, craft, and share stories.

Threads: @thesoundstories

Website: thesoundstories.com

RICHARD J. JONES | Lighting Designer

Richard lit the actor-musician Broadway Production of *Sweeney Todd* at the Eugene O'Neill Theatre in New York, for which he won a Drama Desk Award for Outstanding Lighting Design. He lit the original production of *The Railway Children* at The National Railway Museum in York, and subsequent productions at London Waterloo, Toronto and the purpose-built Kings Cross Theatre where it ran for over two years.

Richard's theatre credits span 35 years and include West End, touring and overseas work. Including: *Only Fools and Horses The Musical, Sunset Boulevard, Sweeney Todd, The Gondoliers, Mack and Mabel* and *Carmen* (West End); *The Children, Cabaret, Jekyll and Hyde, Breaking the Code* and *Venus in Fur* (English Theatre Frankfurt); *Accidental Death of an Anarchist, Crongton Knights, To Kill a Mockingbird, The Diary of Anne Frank, Brideshead Revisited, Beautiful Thing, Wuthering Heights, Rasputin, Candide, All Quiet on the Western Front* (UK Tours). He has recently lit *The Strictly Come Dancing Arena Tour* his twelfth year, *Strictly Professionals Tour* his third year, and is working on designs for *The Wizard of Oz* for Birmingham Old Rep, *Cinderella* for Manchester Opera House and *Jack and the Beanstalk* for Wimbledon Theatre.

Richard is delighted to be lighting *The Whistling* at The Mill at Sonning.

GUY BARRETT | Illusionist

Guy Barrett comes from a show business family background, his father Norman a former Circus Ringmaster and his mother Sally a former professional Ice Skater.

Guy began performing Magic at a very early age and has won many awards as a junior magician, and then numerous awards including the British Ring Shield from the International Brotherhood of Magicians and third place in the Illusion category at FISM (the World Championships of Magic held every four years).

Guy has performed all around the globe performing his Illusion Act and then full Illusion Show, in theatre, TV, theme park, corporate events and circus.

Guy started designing and building illusions in 1992, and now Guy Barrett Illusion Design is the go-to place for Magic Consultancy, Illusion Design, Illusion & Theatrical Props Building and training in all aspects of Magic & Illusion performance and show direction.

Guy lectures on Illusion Design and construction of Illusion Theory, all around the UK Europe and as far away as China.

Guy's knowledge both on the technical side of theatre and the performance side make him sought after by individual magicians and illusionists of all levels and large established companies wanting to embark on ambitious theatrical projects.

PEARSON CASTING CDG CDA CSA | Casting

Pearson Casting CDG CDA CSA are an award-winning, freelance casting house based in London, Liverpool and New York, founded and run by husband and wife team Rosie and James Pearson. In 2022 they won 'Best Casting In Regional Theatre' at the CDG Awards for their work on *RENT*.

Theatre includes: *Titanique* (West End); *Starlight Express* (Troubadour, Wembley); *Six The Musical* (Vaudeville Theatre and UK & International Tour); *Operation Mincemeat* (Fortune Theatre); *Superyou!* (Leicester Curve); *Lizzie* (Hope Mill Theatre); *Fly More Than You Fall* (Southwark Playhouse); *The Whistling* (The Mill at Sonning); *Little Piece of You: An Atypical Musical* (Theatre Royal, Drury Lane); *Chicago* (European Tour); *The Phantom Of The Opera* (International Tour); *Come Alive: The Greatest Showman Circus Spectacular* (Empress Museum); *House of Cleopatra* (Edinburgh Fringe; *Drop Dead Gorgeous* (Edinburgh Fringe); *Play On!* (UK Tour); *Clue* (US Tour); *Pretty Woman: The Musical* (US Tour); *Bluey's Big Play* (Southbank Centre & UK Tour); *42 Balloons* (Lowry Theatre); *Gypsy* and *High Society* (The Mill at Sonning); *Remembrance Monday* (Seven Dials Playhouse); *Christmas Actually* (Southbank Centre); *Lizzie* (Southwark Playhouse & UK Tour); *Police Cops: The Musical* (Southwark Playhouse & UK Tour); *Dolly Parton's Smoky Mountains Christmas Carol* (Queen Elizabeth Hall); *Cherry Jezebel* (Liverpool Everyman Theatre); *RENT* (Hope Mill Theatre); *A Christmas Carol* (Shakespeare North Playhouse); *Horse-Play* (Riverside Studios); *To the Streets* (Birmingham Hippodrome); *Così fan tutte* (London Coliseum); *Unfortunate* (UK Tour); *Lift* (Southwark Playhouse); *Five Guys Named Moe* (Upstairs at the Gatehouse).

TV includes: *Anne* (World Productions & ITV) as Casting Assistant.

Feature Films include: *Crystal* (Xenon Films); *Stephen* (Melanie Manchot).

Short Films include: *The Red Chamber* (Lockbridge Productions); *No Traveller Returns* (Andrew Pennington); *Mummy's Boy* (Typecast Productions); *Wormfood* (Ali Coulson/Sarah Higgins); *Power of Numbers* (Standard Chartered/Liverpool FC).

AMBER EDLIN | Children's Casting

Amber graduated from Guildford School of Acting. As an actor in TV she has been seen in leading roles in *Eastenders*, *Heartbeat*, *Doctors*, *Holby City*, *London's Burning* and *The Sins*. In theatre she has appeared in the West End, Fringe, Touring and here at The Mill at Sonning Theatre where she has played Mavis in *Stepping Out*, Jacqueline in *Don't Dress for Dinner*, Judy in *A Night in Provence* and many more. She has also appeared in films, commercial campaigns and voiceovers. Amber regularly works as an Acting Coach and has an excellent track record of results. She coaches for self-tapes, castings and auditions, as well as teaching the LAMDA syllabus privately and at a number of local schools and performing arts colleges.

She is delighted to have worked on *The Whistling*, developing Mary in casting and in rehearsal workshops with our three chosen young actors.

CHARACTERS

ELSPETH SWANSOME – Elspeth carries the grief of her recently deceased sister with her. She is at a new beginning in her life, but a fish out of water. She has within her an inner strength, but it is only through her developing love for Mary that she can access it.

MARY – Mary is silenced by the threat of violence. This fear is a constant shadow over her. She is weighted by grief. Despite her silence, Mary is clever.

MISS VIOLET GILLIES – Miss Gillies embodies Iskar House – longstanding, stoic in the face of adversity but, beneath the façade, lives something fragile. The scars on her face are a permanent reminder of a troubled past.

GREER – Greer embodies the world-weariness of the island. She works hard for little reward. Life has made her tough, but her love for Mary is genuine, even if she has strange ways of displaying it.

BRIDGET ARGYLE – Bridget takes pride in her role as the minister's wife and enjoys the access it gives her to the islanders and their secrets. Beneath her welcoming and cheery exterior, she is cunning, a plotter.

ROBERT ARGYLE – Robert takes pride in his position as minister on the island. Although compassionate, he is staunchly ideological, and as a community leader, shapes the island around his worldview.

REID PATERSON – Paterson is the island's shop owner. He is frustrated by the lack of opportunity on the island for female company. His approach to young women is uncultured and slightly intimidating. Despite his flaws, Paterson appreciates the beauty of the island.

AILSA – Ailsa is on the outside, thought of as a witch-like woman. She takes no part in the church, having put her beliefs in nature. She is as weather-beaten as the island itself. Beneath her slight eccentricity is a caring and loyal soul.

HETTIE – The spirit of Hettie appears through song and movement. She is a young woman, broken by the island.

DOCTOR
SHADOWS OF ISKAR HOUSE
SPIRITS
ISLANDERS

SETTING

The Island of Skelthsea. A fictional Scottish Island. 1860.

AUTHORS' NOTES

Shadows of Iskar House are non-literal, non-speaking shadows of the house. They move gracefully and balletically and are unseen by the characters. They are at one with their environment; they are at one with the music and dialogue.

The shadows, spirits and all other roles should be played by members of the company.

With grateful thanks to: Rebecca Netley; Dan Usztan; Adam Rolston; Sally Hughes; Joe Pitcher; Ben Keiper and the team at Concord; and our actors, creative team and crew.

ACT ONE

(Seagulls scream and cry. Waves break on rocks. A whistling wind.)

(Finally, darkness begins to fall, the gulls fade away, leaving us with the sounds of the waves.)

Scene One

(A Scottish folk/shanty song is sung by the cast.)

*(**HETTIE** alone. Deep in the sea. She floats, dances, balletic and beautiful. Something violent arrests her movements.)*

(Sounds of a steam boat. A boat's bell.)

*(**HETTIE** disappears.)*

(The Island of Skelthsea.)

(Late evening. Darkness. Mist. Waves against the shore.)

*(In the mist, a woman appears, holding an oil lamp. **GREER**.)*

(A boatsman/woman appears, throws a rope over the mooring post.)

(Passengers begin to hoist themselves up onto the island. They are wrapped in coats, hats and hoods. They carry cases, oil lanterns.)

*(A young woman, **ELSPETH SWANSOME**, carrying a single case, climbs up onto the island. She is not used to boats.)*

(She puts down her case, unsure where to go.)

ELSPETH. *(To one of the disembarked passengers.)* Excuse me, do you –

> *(But the passenger is too focused on his/her own business to notice.)*

*(Through the thick mist, **GREER** sees **ELSPETH**. A sense of foreboding. Unwelcoming.)*

GREER. Miss Swansome.

ELSPETH. *(Uncertain.)* Good evening? Miss Gillies?

GREER. *(Stony, unsmiling.)* Miss Gillies is back at the house.

ELSPETH. Oh. Thank you for meeting me. I'm Elspeth. Elspeth Swansome.

GREER. It's this way.

*(**ELSPETH** picks up her case. It's heavy. **GREER** does not offer to help.)*

ELSPETH. Is it far to the house?

GREER. I expect you're used to carriages in the city.

ELSPETH. No, I –

GREER. Everywhere's a walk on the island.

ELSPETH. How long have you been on the island, Mrs...?

GREER. My name's Greer. I've been here all my life.

ELSPETH. And you live at Iskar House?

*(**GREER** grunts her assent.)*

So you know Miss Gillies well?

...And Mary?

GREER. Watch your step. It can be treacherous round here. The whole island can be at dark.

*(**ELSPETH** already having second thoughts.)*

ELSPETH. What's it like? Living on the island, I mean.

GREER. If you can't fit in, you'll get lonely.

ELSPETH. I believe loneliness is something you carry with you.

GREER. Well, I hope you're not carrying too much. There's more than enough here as it is.

ELSPETH. Do...do the boats come back often to the island?

(**GREER** *stops and looks at* **ELSPETH.**)

GREER. You'll be able to leave soon enough. They always do.

Right, nearly there.

Try not to stare, when you meet Miss Gillies.

ELSPETH. Why would I stare?

GREER. Everyone stares.

(*Lights up on the interior of Iskar House.*)

(**ELSPETH** *and* **GREER** *are now face-to-face with* **MISS GILLIES***. She is clearly hiding one side of her face from* **ELSPETH** *[and from us]. She wears a medical mask on the hidden side of her face.*)

Scene Two

(Iskar House. Continuing from Scene One.)

(Iskar House is a burnt-out house. The characters, however, see it as opulent, well-furnished, except for **MISS GILLIES**, *who sees the house in its burnt-out state.)*

MISS GILLIES. Greer, take Elspeth's case up to her room, please.

ELSPETH. Oh, no. I can –

MISS GILLIES. *(Assertively.)* Miss Swansome…has hours of travelling behind her. *(To* **ELSPETH**.*)* I can see you're tired.

I'm Violet Gillies. Mary's aunt.

ELSPETH. Elspeth.

MISS GILLIES. Iskar House doesn't always appear the most welcoming; we don't waste light, and it's too big for those of us who remain. But you are welcome, Elspeth. Hettie chose a bad time to leave us.

ELSPETH. Hettie. Was she the previous nanny?

> *(***GREER*** is hanging on a bit too long, eavesdropping.)*

MISS GILLIES. Thank you, Greer.

> *(Displeased to be excluded,* **GREER** *exits with* **ELSPETH**'s *case.)*

ELSPETH. I was very sorry to read of little William's passing. Poor Mary. To lose her mother and then her brother.

You didn't say in your correspondence exactly how he –

MISS GILLIES. What Mary needs more than anything is to look to the future. She has suffered far too much grief to spend her time wallowing in the past.

From your correspondence I gather you, too, have lost those close to you.

ELSPETH. I had a sister. Clara. She –

> (**MISS GILLIES** *involuntarily touches her face.* **ELSPETH** *sees the medical mask [as do we]. It surprises* **ELSPETH**.)

(Trying to recompose herself.) Perhaps...perhaps you're right. It doesn't do to live in the past.

MISS GILLIES. No need to be abashed, Elspeth. There was a fire here at Iskar House when I was sixteen. I was badly burned. I'm accustomed to the response this brings [face mask].

ELSPETH. I'm sorry, I didn't mean to –

MISS GILLIES. If it's any consolation, I feel as much guilt for causing awkwardness in people as they do for displaying it.

As for your own grief, it gives me no pleasure, of course, but I do wonder if you're perhaps better equipped to deal with Mary. I'm not used to children and their –

You look lost already.

ELSPETH. I'm just trying to imagine myself here.

MISS GILLIES. I expect to you this house seems lavish. These paintings and wall hangings. The polished furniture.

> *(There are no paintings, wall hangings or polished furniture in the set.)*

ELSPETH. It's all very lovely.

MISS GILLIES. To some, maybe. Years may have passed since the fire and restoration. But still, all I see is the black skeleton of the house. The charred timber, the singed furniture.

> *(This affects **ELSPETH**. Lost to her own thoughts. Touching the burnt timbers.)*

Well. Best not to dwell.

> *(Beat.)*

ELSPETH. You've shown faith in me. I... I hope I'm equal to the task.

Will I meet Mary this evening?

MISS GILLIES. Mary's at rest now. But you'll meet her in the morning. Elspeth, there's something I need to tell you about Mary. I didn't mention it in our correspondence because I thought it might dissuade any prospective nanny – there's not many would want to leave the bustle of Edinburgh for the likes of here.

ELSPETH. And what is it, Miss Gillies?

MISS GILLIES. ...Since the death of her brother, Mary hasn't spoken a word. We've tried and tried. I've offered rewards; I've tried punishing her. But not a word passes her lips.

She has been seen by a doctor from the mainland. He seems to think...

> *(A new presence should be felt.)*

Is that you, Greer?

> *(Silence.)*

The house certainly has its creaks and cracks.

ELSPETH. What about the doctor?

MISS GILLIES. At first, he thought her condition would be temporary. But it has persisted longer than anyone imagined.

> *(From a surprising entrance, **MARY** appears. **MARY** is nine years old. She wears her nightdress and holds an old, tatty, cloth doll [Bobbity]. Her entrance is unseen by **ELSPETH** and **MISS GILLIES**.)*

If she doesn't improve, there's a facility on the mainland that the doctor recommends.

ELSPETH. An asylum?

MISS GILLIES. Perhaps your being here will help her to avoid –

> *(Seeing **MARY**.)*

Oh, Mary. What are you doing up?

MARY. ...

MISS GILLIES. Have you been sleepwalking again?

*(To **ELSPETH**.)* She does this from time to time. And we find her somewhere in the house. She has no idea how she got there.

(Quietly. Tentatively.) Mary, this is –

> *(Suddenly, loudly, **GREER** comes running down the stairs.)*

GREER. Mary's out of her room! Miss Gillies, Mary –

MISS GILLIES. She's here, Greer.

> *(**GREER** stops. Relieved.)*

> *(Beat.)*

ELSPETH. Mary, I'm Elspeth. Your aunt has asked me to come to stay here with you all. I hope you and I will have lots of fun.

MISS GILLIES. *(To* **MARY**.*)* This is the lady I told you about.

ELSPETH. *(Smiling, at* **MARY**.*)* I'm relying on you to show me around the island. I've always wanted to go fossil hunting. You'll have to teach me.

MARY. …

MISS GILLIES. Elspeth's from Edinburgh.

ELSPETH. And who's this, Mary?

> (**MARY** *clutches Bobbity more tightly.*)

MISS GILLIES. That's Bobbity. You'll rarely see her without it.

ELSPETH. Well, it's nice to meet you, Bobbity.

> (**ELSPETH** *stands alone.*)

> (*The sound of a whistle. Eerie. Haunting.* **ELSPETH** *unsettled.*)

MISS GILLIES. Right, let's get you back to bed.

ELSPETH. I could take –

GREER. I'll do it. Come on, Mary.

> (**GREER** *takes* **MARY** *by the hand, and they exit.*)

> (**ELSPETH** *and* **MISS GILLIES** *alone.*)

ELSPETH. I think Greer doesn't like me very much. I don't know if I accidentally offended –

MISS GILLIES. You'll get used to her. There's a lot to get used to here. Let me show you to your room. You'll need your sleep.

> (**ELSPETH** *and* **MISS GILLIES** *exit.*)

> (*A soft musical wind blows over the island and through the cracks and windows of the house.*)

(A ghostly curtain billows in the wind of an open window.)

(Suddenly, **ELSPETH** *and* **MISS GILLIES** *enter through a doorway. We are now in* **ELSPETH***'s room.)*

(Mid conversation.) All the rooms we use are this side of the house. Please don't go to the East Wing. We call that William's wing. He used to like playing there. But it's in disrepair. The salt water from the sea corrodes everything on an island like this. This will be your room.

ELSPETH. Is this where Mary's previous nanny slept?

MISS GILLIES. *(Almost too quickly.)* No.

No, she was upstairs. I think this room is warmer. You have everything here you need, I believe. And we'll see you for breakfast.

(**MISS GILLIES** *goes to leave.*)

ELSPETH. But Miss Gillies –

(**MISS GILLIES** *turns back.*)

Mary. What...how would you like me to proceed?

MISS GILLIES. When Hettie left us, Mary took it badly. She needs to laugh again. She loves to walk on the beach, to see the seals and the gulls.

ELSPETH. And schooling?

MISS GILLIES. I have her for lessons in the morning. You'll look after her till bedtime. Although she doesn't talk, she is clever. Very clever.

(**MISS GILLIES** *goes to leave.*)

ELSPETH. And...

(**MISS GILLIES** *turns again. Growing impatient.*)

I'm sorry.

MISS GILLIES. What else?

ELSPETH. No one has told me exactly why the previous nanny left in such a hurry.

MISS GILLIES. Hettie vanished without a word of goodbye. Not to me. Not to the children. Why she did so… You'd have to ask her.

Goodnight, Elspeth.

(**MISS GILLIES** *exits.*)

(**ELSPETH** *stands alone.*)

(*She unpacks her clothes into a drawer. In the drawer she finds something. A stone wrapped in hair. Music indicates the weirdness of this.*)

(*As she holds it, the hair unravels and the stone drops loudly on the floor. A slight shock for* **ELSPETH**. *And then the weirdness of holding some long stands of hair. She re-wraps the stone in the hair. She throws it out of the opened window, and closes it.*)

(**ELSPETH** *finishes her unpacking.*)

(*The sound of a whistle. Eerie.* **ELSPETH** *stops what she's doing. Suddenly, she feels cold. She listens.*)

(*Creaks from above. More noises.*)

(*A lullaby is softly hummed from somewhere. Intermittent, from various places:*)

HETTIE.
> I WALK WITH MY LITTLE LANTERN
> MY LANTERN MYSELF AND I
> IN HEAVEN THE STARS ARE SHINING
> DOWN HERE WE'RE STARS TO THE SKY.

ELSPETH. Mary? Is that you?

> *(Silence. **ELSPETH** takes off her shoes. Puts them beside her bed. She takes off her locket, regards it tenderly, then puts it in her shoe.)*

> *(She hears more creaks.)*

Greer?

> *(She hears someone singing snatches of the lullaby. Increasingly eerie.)*

> *(**ELSPETH** goes looking. Out of her room.)*

> *(Goes back to her room.)*

> *(The window is open again. How is that possible? The curtain flapping. Again, she closes it, decisively this time.)*

> *(Sits on her bed.)*

> *(She reaches for her locket, but she already took it off. She reaches for her shoes – but they have been moved. She's confused. We should share in this confusion; the shoes have definitely moved.)*

> *(She takes out her locket. Opens it. Looks at it. Kisses the picture.)*

I love you.

> *(Puts the locket back.)*

(Slowly, darkness falls.)

(Allows herself to fall asleep.)

(Music. **HOUSE SHADOWS** *enter, lightly, beautifully. The roaring of flames.* **ELSPETH** *dreams of a house fire.)*

(Beat.)

(Suddenly, seagulls scream. Morning light pours in. The sound of waves and gulls.)

Scene Three

(The beach. Waves and wind. Gulls screaming.)

*(**ELSPETH** and **MARY** enter, walking slowly along the beach. **ELSPETH** trying very hard to connect with **MARY**.)*

ELSPETH. It's good to be out of the house a while, isn't it?

MARY. …

ELSPETH. I love how the tide washes the sand endlessly new. A clean start.

> *(**MARY** stops to consider this.)*

Now, Mary. Your aunt says you are not normally allowed sweets, but I think we can allow ourselves a little treat, don't you?

MARY. …

ELSPETH. *(Taking wrapped sweets from a pocket.)* Let's see. These are chocolate, and these are toffee. Which do you prefer?

> *(**MARY** shrugs.)*

I know. Have this one now, and let's put the other in your pocket for later.

> *(As **ELSPETH** goes to put the sweet in **MARY**'s pocket, **MARY** flinches away.)*

> *(Beat.)*

> *(**ELSPETH** tries to take it in her stride.)*

Here. Save it for later.

> *(**MARY** puts the sweet in her own pocket.)*

Oh, look. They're tying up the boats; does that mean they're expecting a storm? Look at the clouds forming.

(*They stop and look out at the sea.*)

Your aunt said that you like to watch the seals. I've only ever seen them in pictures. Do you see many from here?

(**MARY** *points.*)

On those rocks? Where that man's fishing?

Oh dear. I think he thought I was waving at him.

(**ELSPETH** *trying hard. But already running out of things to say.*)

And the birds. Your aunt said you like the...

(*But* **MARY** *has wandered to the sea. She picks a stone off the beach and, inexpertly, throws it into the sea.*)

(**ELSPETH** *re-joins* **MARY**.)

I don't know the names of many birds, I'm afraid. (*Pointing.*) I think they might be... Are they swallows?

(**MARY** *has no response.*)

(**ELSPETH** *defeated.*)

I understand you were close to your previous nanny. I ... I wonder how you ever communicated.

(**MARY** *turns away.*)

No. I'm not trying to get you to speak.

(**MARY** *turns back.*)

I'll never ask you to speak simply because...because it's easier for the adults. Mary, when I received the letter from your aunt explaining that you lost your mother last year and then your brother so recently... I knew that you and I shared something, something that lives within the silence inside us. You see, I lost my sister not long ago. And she whom I had grown up with and cared for when she was sick and played with and read stories with and, oh, all sorts of nameless and endless things, would never come back to me.

I can't make William return. But if I can help you through what I went through when Clara died, I will give you my all.

> (**MARY** *is listening.*)

> (**ELSPETH** *smiles a sad smile.*)

You can speak to me anytime you want to, but I promise, I will never ask you to.

> (**MARY** *bends down and writes something with her finger in the sand. When she is finished,* **ELSPETH** *leans over to read.*)

"Swifts"... (?)

Oh, they're swifts!

> (**ELSPETH** *and* **MARY** *look up to the sky.*)

I can see I'm going to learn a lot from you. I bet there are things all along this beach you could show me.

> (*She looks along the beach, into the distance.*)

I wonder what that woman's doing? Do you see? Where the sea meets the sand. She looks like she's collecting something. A treasure hunter, maybe.

> (*Suddenly, a man enters. He holds fishing tackle and has a few dead fish hanging from hooks [macabre]. He is* **REID PATERSON**.)

PATERSON. So...*you're* the new nanny at the big house...

>   (**PATERSON** *looks* **ELSPETH** *up and down.*)

>   (**ELSPETH** *nods and pulls her coat tighter.*)

I'm Reid Paterson. I own the shop. Anything you need...or *want*...just come by.

ELSPETH. Thank you. *(Calling.)* Mary...

PATERSON. Have you got any word from her yet?

ELSPETH. I'm sure she'll speak when she's ready. We're just on our walk, so...

Come on Mary.

>   (**ELSPETH** *begins to walk away, but* **PATERSON** *puts a hand on her.*)

PATERSON. You didn't tell me your name.

ELSPETH. El– Miss Swansome. I think we'll be late for church if we don't keep –

PATERSON. The last one. Hettie. She was very pretty. But she told lies. *(He moves in too close.)* Lies on an island like this are poison.

ELSPETH. Well. I'm neither pretty nor a liar, so the island will be spared. Come Mary.

PATERSON. Oh, look. It's the last of the Bo'ness Witches.

>   (**PATERSON** *points to the woman in the distance. She is* **AILSA**.*)

I'd make a run for it before she puts a spell on you.

I'll look out for you, *Elspeth*, at the shop.

>   (**ELSPETH** *watches him leave in silent discomfort. When she turns back, the woman is picking up seaweed.*)

(**MARY** *goes towards the woman and picks up a few bits of seaweed. She passes them tentatively to* **AILSA**.)

AILSA. We call that seaweed sea lettuce. Fry it up with onions and salt. Does you good.

(**ELSPETH** *joins them.*)

ELSPETH. Are you helping, Mary?

AILSA. Oh, so, you're the new nanny.

ELSPETH. So everybody tells me.

AILSA. Hm, well, there aren't many secrets on the island. Much as people try to keep them.

I'm Ailsa. The people on Skelthsea have different names for me, of course. They think I don't know. But I know.

What have you got there, Mary?

(**MARY** *shows her a shell.*)

Ah, a turritella shell. It's a gift from the moon, did you know that? As the moon pulls the sea towards her, the sea leaves these treasures for us to find. And this one was left for you.

Look, the colouration here. Unusual. It could almost be an M. Just for you, Mary.

(**MARY** *shrugs and throws the shell back in the sea.*)

Maybe it'll find its way back to you. These things often do.

(**ELSPETH** *looking for a change of subject.*)

ELSPETH. ...What do you do with the seaweed?

AILSA. They keep inventing all these medicines, but the ones the earth gives us are the only ones I'll trust. If ever you're in need of a remedy, I'll have something for you. Something natural.

Are you two on your way to church?

ELSPETH. We took the long way around so Mary could show me the beach. Will we see you at church?

AILSA. I don't go to the church. Not anymore.

ELSPETH. Oh… Oh. Well –

AILSA. You could call in. My cottage is just up there. Come, I'll show you. Just up and around beyond the sheep fold.

ELSPETH. Well, we're heading that way [different way], I think, so…

> (**AILSA** *takes* **ELSPETH** *by the sleeve. Very uncomfortable.*)

AILSA. You'll come to visit me.

ELSPETH. *(Trying for politeness.)* Oh. Yes. That would be – [nice]

AILSA. No. You *will* come to visit me.

ELSPETH. I don't…

AILSA. When you need someone to tell.

ELSPETH. *(Confused.)* Tell what?

AILSA. All is not well at Iskar House.

> (**AILSA** *lets* **ELSPETH**'*s arm go and exits.*)

> (**ELSPETH** *is unsettled.*)

ELSPETH. *(To* **MARY**.*)* Come along now. We don't want to be late.

> (*Church music begins to play.*)

> (**ELSPETH** *and* **MARY** *exit.*)

Scene Four

(Church music continues.)

(Change of light takes us into a dark, atmospheric church.)

(Entering the church, the entire cast becomes the congregation. They join the music in song. A solemn hymn.)

(Each cast member carries an oil lamp. On entrance, each cast member positions their lamp on the back wall and then takes their position for the church service.)

(When all the oil lamps have been set in position, they should create the Christan cross.)

*(Positioning himself before the cross, **ROBERT ARGYLE**.)*

*(Last to enter are **ELSPETH** and **MARY**.)*

(When the hymn finishes.)

ROBERT. In recent times, grief has befallen this island. And we must soften our hearts towards those in mourning. And while it is difficult, we must cherish grief, for it is an expression of our love. We should welcome that God has acted in his wisdom – whether we understand it or not.

> *(A whistling wind begins to pick up.)*

But we must not be swayed by our grief. Never should we turn ourselves to the necromancer or the medium. Leviticus forbids it. Isiah forbids it. Timothy forbids it. John forbids it. I could go on. There is but one mediator between man and God and that is our Lord, His Son, who gave himself for us. Amen.

CONGREGATION. Amen.

ROBERT. We have seen the result of this kind of wickedness on our island: sacrilegious commune with dark spirits. Animal sacrifices. Unholy rock formations. "Woe unto to the wicked," says our book, "for the reward of his hands shall be given to him." And so it *was* done to him.

PARISHIONER. *(Audible whisper.)* And just a child...

ROBERT. We are all but children before our Lord and we must all take responsibility for our actions.

But we must also face the future, and new tides bring new faces. And this is the strength of our island. The open-hearted manner in which we greet those from distant horizons.

> *(All heads turn to look at **ELSPETH**. A whistling wind. The storm intensifying.)*

Well, it sounds like *somebody* [God] thinks I've gone on long enough. Before we make for our suppers, please join me in a gesture of peace to one another. Peace be with you.

CONGREGATION. And also with you.

ROBERT. Please, ladies and gentlemen, watch your footing on the paths back. We all know too well how dangerous it can be this time of year.

> *(Church music plays. Church goers hum the hymn as they take their lanterns and exit.)*

> *(**ELSPETH** is last to leave.)*

> *(As **ELSPETH** is about to exit, the minister, **ROBERT**, goes after her.)*

ROBERT. Miss Swansome?

(ELSPETH turns.)

ROBERT. Miss Swansome, I was hoping to meet you. I'm Robert Argyle, the minister, as you see.

(A kindly lady from the congregation joins them. She is BRIDGET ARGYLE.)

Oh, and this is my wife...

BRIDGET. Bridget Argyle. Pleased to meet you.

(ELSPETH is cautious, but shakes hands.)

ROBERT. Coming from the mainland, we must seem very rural to you.

ELSPETH. In Edinburgh, I could walk the streets all day and no would know who I am. Here, everyone seems to know my name before I have had a chance to introduce myself.

BRIDGET. That's Skelthsea for you. Gossip and whispers do travel. In fact, whenever I *can't* hear the gossiping, I assume they must be gossiping about me.

ROBERT. Still, I hope you won't find our lives here too incestuous.

BRIDGET. *(Admonishingly.)* Robert.

ROBERT. I just meant –

BRIDGET. I know what you meant. Why don't you fetch our coats? The storm's right over us.

(ROBERT leaves.)

BRIDGET. And Miss Gillies... she has made you welcome, I hope?

ELSPETH. Very much so. But...

But I do not please Greer, somehow.

(BRIDGET smiles.)

BRIDGET. *(Confidentially.)* Greer... Greer is a complicated soul.

ELSPETH. I'm not sure our personal complications should preclude courtesy.

(This pleases **BRIDGET**.*)*

BRIDGET. You're an educated girl. But you've endured much, haven't you? It's in your eyes.

ELSPETH. *(Attempting stoicism.)* I'm sure we all have to contend with grief at one time or another.

BRIDGET. Be gentle with yourself, Miss Swansome. The people on this island take care of each other. And Robert and I will look out for you.

ELSPETH. Thank you.

BRIDGET. How's little Mary? I used to take her for French lessons, you know. At Iskar House.

ELSPETH. But no longer?

BRIDGET. Not since William...not since William passed. Miss Gillies wanted to ease the pressure on Mary. Understandable. And of course...when she stopped speaking, it made it very difficult.

Is there any hope for her, do you think?

ELSPETH. I don't know. I've only just begun with her but –

(The storm intensifies, interrupting **ELSPETH**.*)*

I should get back to the house.

BRIDGET, But come for tea soon. We're just in the manse there. It's lovely to see a new face on Skelthsea.

ELSPETH. *(Non-committedly.)* Thank you.

BRIDGET. Elspeth. It's a genuine offer. Come for a slice of cake when you have some time to yourself.

ELSPETH. Thank you.

BRIDGET. What cake do you like?

ELSPETH. *(Smiling.)* I'm yet to meet a cake I didn't like.

       *(***ELSPETH** *exits.)*

Scene Five

(Iskar House. Daylight.)

(The lightest underscoring of music.)

*(**HOUSE SHADOWS** are part of the scene's breath and heartbeat.)*

*(**MARY** enters. She holds Bobbity by the arm. She is silent.)*

*(**HOUSE SHADOWS** represent hiding and seeking.)*

*(**MARY** pads around, furtively. She is looking for something/someone.)*

(Finally, she looks underneath the staircase.)

(Tension/atmosphere builds.)

*(**ELSPETH** emerges.)*

ELSPETH. *(Playfully.)* Ah, you found me! Well done.

Right. Now it's your turn to hide. Are you ready?

*(**MARY** nods.)*

I'll close my eyes and begin counting.

*(**ELSPETH** turns away and covers her eyes. **HOUSE SHADOWS** exit. **MARY** exits quickly, silently, and without **ELSPETH** realising.)*

And I promise not to cheat.

(Playfully.) I *did* wonder if you and Bobbity had accidentally missed a few numbers. You found me very – [quickly].

(She turns to **MARY**. *But* **MARY** *has gone.)*

(Aware of her aloneness.)

*(***ELSPETH***, rather than counting, sits. A moment of noticeable reprieve.* **ELSPETH** *allows us to see how tired she has grown. The underscoring music should delineate her reverie.)*

(A little weather plays against the house.)

*(***ELSPETH*** *in deep thought.)*

(For **MARY** *to hear.)* "Thirty-two, thirty-three, thirty-four..."

(Back to sitting in silence.)

(Musical underscoring continues to represent the melancholia of **ELSPETH**'s *thoughts.)*

*(***ELSPETH*** *takes out her locket and opens it. She studies the picture inside. Touches it.)*

(Playfully.) "Sixty-six, sixty-seven..."

(A final longing look at the picture in her locket.)

(She gives the locket a kiss, tucks it back in.)

Ninety-eight, ninety-nine. Ready or not, here I come...

*(***ELSPETH*** *begins looking around.)*

*(***HOUSE SHADOWS*** *enter, hiding and seeking. The whole house is in a ballet of soft movement.)*

(Musical underscoring.)

*(Whenever **ELSPETH** exits in her search, **MARY** may enter. Hiding behind the various items of furniture and **HOUSE SHADOWS**.)*

Now, where would a small girl hide in a house as big as this?

I wonder if a clever girl might make a hiding place of...

*(**ELSPETH** opens a door...)*

...here!

(But there is no one there.)

(Silence.)

*(**ELSPETH** hears a creak.)*

Ah, you see the trouble with an old house like this one, is it might be very good for hiding places, but creaky stairs and creaky boards give away the lightest of feet.

*(**ELSPETH** looks around. Nothing.)*

Hmm. Not just a good seeker, but a good hider, too. Very well...

*(Still looking, she begins to worry that she has really lost **MARY**.)*

All right, Mary. I'm going to try one more room and if I haven't found you, I'll declare you the winner.

*(**ELSPETH** looks for five seconds. Nothing.)*

Well done. You and Bobbity are the winners. Why don't you come and collect your prize?

*(**ELSPETH** still looking. Growing more concerned.)*

I think the winner certainly deserves at least one chocolate. *(Going into her pockets.)*

(But still no MARY.)

Mary. I'm asking you to come out now, please.

(The sound of footsteps.)

*(**ELSPETH** creeps tentatively towards the locked door to William's wing.)*

Mary, if you've gone in here, you know that's out of bounds.

*(**ELSPETH** stops at the threshold to William's wing. She tries the door. Locked.)*

If you've managed to get in there, it's time to come out now –

(A distant noise from somewhere else.)

(To herself.) Oh, so you're not in William's wing. Sounds as if you're upstairs.

*(**ELSPETH** takes us into **HETTIE**'s room.)*

(We hear footsteps, as if someone is running away, hiding.)

*(**ELSPETH** is unsettled but trying to hide it.)*

Mary?

*(**ELSPETH** thinks she has found her when she hears a noise from somewhere. But there is no one there.)*

(To herself.) I don't know where you are.

(Music underscores.)

*(**ELSPETH** sits on the bed. Finds a hairbrush. A few strands of long hair.)*

(She picks up a weird doll. When she turns the doll around to see its face.)

(A noise.)

*(**ELSPETH** finds a small, makeshift doorway.)*

Mary?

*(Tension builds as **ELSPETH** braces herself for what might lie behind the strange door.)*

(She opens it.)

*(Crouched inside a dark cubbyhole, a small figure. Slowly **MARY** looks up. Her face is lit by a candle. Dark shadows. **ELSPETH** scared.)*

(Trying not to betray her anger.) Oh, Mary.

However was I supposed to find you?

Come out of there, please.

*(**ELSPETH** gives **MARY** her hand, and **MARY** comes out.)*

Now, I did promise a chocolate for the winner. One for you and one for Bobbity. Here.

*(**ELSPETH** passes **MARY** a wrapped chocolate. When **MARY** takes it, **ELSPETH** sees something in **MARY**'s hand.)*

*(**ELSPETH** recoils, shocked. Music should indicate the shock.)*

Mary, what is that?

*(**MARY** holds it out. A stone wrapped in hair.)*

Where did you find this?!

MARY. ...

ELSPETH. I found this stone in my room on my first day here. This hair wrapped around it. I threw this out into the overgrowth outside my room. How did you ever...?

(**MARY** *feels as if she is being told off.*)

Oh, no, Mary. It's all right. I'm not angry. I just...

Come on.

This is Hettie's room, isn't it? Did you and William play in here with her?

(**MARY** *nods.*)

And is that Hettie's doll?

(**ELSPETH** *points to the doll, but it's gone.*)

(*Suddenly,* **MISS GILLIES** *enters.*)

MISS GILLIES. There you two are. I've been looking all over for you.

ELSPETH. Sorry, Miss Gillies, we've been playing hide and seek. (*Including* **MARY**.) Although I'm no match for Mary. She has an uncanny ability to find me. And knows all the best hiding places.

MISS GILLIES. I hope you haven't been hiding in William's wing. You know it's –

ELSPETH. No. Mary knows to leave William's wing untouched. We both do.

MISS GILLIES. Mary, could you go and help Greer in the kitchen for a moment?

(**MARY** *exits.*)

(*Only,* **MARY** *doesn't really exit. She hides and continues to listen.*)

This is Hettie's room.

ELSPETH. I thought so.

MISS GILLIES. Hettie complained of the drafts. We should keep the door closed.

> (**ELSPETH** *wants to say something but holds her tongue.*)

Is that all right, Miss Swansome?

ELSPETH. You've been very welcoming, Miss Gillies. And I'm doing my best with Mary. There are occasional cracks of light, but she returns so little. I wonder if I'm really the –

> (**ELSPETH** *suddenly sees something. It takes her breath away. The doll has returned!*)

MISS GILLIES. What is it?

ELSPETH. The doll. How...?

MISS GILLIES. Hettie must have left it behind.

ELSPETH. I feel there are secrets here. I do not like to ask, but –

MISS GILLIES. There's no secret.

ELSPETH. But, William's wing. You say it is in disrepair. No one goes in there, but I hear noises. And Hettie, she seems to have left such a mark on the island, and yet no one can explain why she left... Is there something I should know?

MISS GILLIES. We have to concentrate on...on those who remain.

ELSPETH. *(Showing her frustration.)* And Greer? I have been nothing but polite and still she seeks to intimidate me. On my first night here, someone moved my shoes. Such a strange thing to do.

MISS GILLIES. There's nothing to worry about.

ELSPETH. And William. Everyone tiptoes around even the mention of his name. There isn't a single picture of him. None of his things. It's as if he never existed. Miss Gillies, if there's something I should know, I believe I deserve to know it.

MISS GILLIES. Nothing is being kept from you, so you needn't go interfering where you're not needed. But there is something I came to tell you. The doctor is coming tomorrow. He'll be assessing Mary – to see if she's made any improvements.

ELSPETH. And has she? In your opinion, since he last saw her?

MISS GILLIES. Mary is not quite herself, not quite in her own mind, is she, Elspeth?

ELSPETH. She's experienced so much death, so much loss. Is there a prescribed manner in which she *should* respond?

MISS GILLIES. To go so long without speaking. You must surely agree she needs help.

ELSPETH. I believe love and kindness are the help she needs.

MISS GILLIES. We must allow the *doctor* to instruct us on how to proceed.

(**MISS GILLIES** *is pricked by a thought.*)

I'm sure he won't need to speak to you, but if he does, what do you think you would offer?

ELSPETH. If I'm of service, I shall simply tell him the truth, that Mary is as any child who enjoys playing and exploring. That she is dealing with her grief by choosing not to speak is just one attribute, not her defining one.

(*Beat.*)

MISS GILLIES. I think it would be better if you answer any questions with brevity and leave any diagnosis to the doctor.

> (**ELSPETH** *and* **MISS GILLIES** *exit, unaware of* **MARY**.)

> (**MARY** *comes out from her hiding place. She picks up the doll. Cradles it to her. We hear the lullaby being sung from offstage.* **MARY** *looks to where the lullaby is coming from. Unsettled. She turns and exits in the other direction.*)

Scene Six

(The manse. A coffin on a trestle. **ROBERT** *and* **AILSA** *by it.* **ROBERT** *pays* **AILSA** *during the following.)*

(Separately, **ELSPETH** *and* **BRIDGET** *approach the manse.)*

ELSPETH. There's so much open space here on Skelthsea and yet, it can feel so oppressive.

ROBERT. For your services.

BRIDGET. And how is Greer treating you now?

ELSPETH. I'm afraid she is yet to thaw towards me.

BRIDGET. Greer is as stubborn as knotweed. She'll come round in her own time.

AILSA. Death keeps us both in business, I suppose.

BRIDGET. Here, come this way. We have the house to ourselves.

Oh.

> *(***ELSPETH** *and* **BRIDGET** *enter the manse, to see* **ROBERT** *and* **AILSA**. *Everyone stops as if caught doing something.* **AILSA** *quickly puts the money in her pocket.)*

ROBERT. I wasn't expecting you back so soon.

BRIDGET. Mrs Paterson couldn't face lunch. *(Amused.)* Her bunions have defeated her, today.

I met Elspeth outside.

ELSPETH. I just came by to see Bridget. I can come back another –

ROBERT. Don't be silly. Welcome. Have you met Ailsa?

AILSA. We passed on the beach. How is your charge?

ELSPETH. She's –

AILSA. Good, good. Well, I'll leave you to it.

> (**AILSA** *leaves.* **ROBERT** *makes to follow.*)

ELSPETH. Please don't leave on my account.

ROBERT. We're just about finished here. Ailsa was just helping me prepare Mr Hamilton.

> (**ROBERT** *insensitively pats the coffin.*)

His family are calling by to discuss the funeral arrangements.

ELSPETH. Oh, I'm sorry...

BRIDGET. No, don't worry. It was only old Angus Hamilton. He should have died years ago. The good Lord ran out of excuses not to take him. What have you there?

ELSPETH. *(Opening a box.)* I picked up some cake from the shop.

BRIDGET. I promised *you* cake.

ROBERT. Ooh.

BRIDGET. Won't the Hamiltons be waiting for you?

> (**ROBERT** *sighs, exits.*)

> (**ELSPETH** *and* **BRIDGET** *glad to be alone.*)

ELSPETH. Are you busy?

BRIDGET. I've hymn books to put out for this evening's service and a few other...

Is everything all right, Elspeth?

> (**ELSPETH** *can't find her words.*)

Is it not working out with Mary?

ELSPETH.   It's more difficult than I imagined. And everybody on the island is judging me by my success... or my failure with Mary.

BRIDGET.   Whatever you think of the islanders, they all wish Mary the best. Her mother, Evangeline, was very well thought of. She and I were good friends.

ELSPETH.   Oh...

She must have been young to die.

BRIDGET.   It wasn't an easy death. She always had a weak chest. Perhaps she needed a warmer climate. A fever took her in the end.

Is there something that troubles you?

ELSPETH.   Bridget, I... I was wondering if you could tell me about William. Miss Gillies closes down conversation anytime his name is mentioned. What kind of accident did he meet?

BRIDGET.   They haven't told you? I can't say I'm surprised. Violet – Miss Gillies is very private. But it's no secret.

There's a cliff to the east. Stack Mor. We always tell the children not to go up there, but... William was quite an explorer. The whole island came out in search. It was two days before Robert found the body.

ELSPETH.   Your husband found him?

BRIDGET.   He's no stranger to seeing dead bodies, of course, but William certainly affected him.

ELSPETH.   Did Mary see it?

BRIDGET.   No. Thank goodness. After Hettie left, you'd often see William exploring all by himself.

ELSPETH.   So, if Hettie hadn't left, William might still be alive.

BRIDGET.   Best not to dwell on it.

ELSPETH. *(Angry with* **HETTIE**.*)* But you must see it as selfish.

BRIDGET. Elspeth, we can't hold it against Hettie for moving on. She was just living her own life. You may find your sympathies align with hers the longer you stay here.

ELSPETH. But she abandoned them while they were still grieving for their mother. What was so pressing that she had to go so suddenly?

BRIDGET. Well, I'm not one for gossip. But...

(Seeing the bag/box.) Are those chocolate slices?

ELSPETH. I couldn't resist. I'm sure the bakery will be my downfall, here.

BRIDGET. Let me get some plates and the tea.

> *(***BRIDGET** *now fussing with teapot, plates, etc.)*

But whenever the supply boats arrive here, Hettie would always be seen befriending the men.

ELSPETH. Are you saying she ran off with someone from the mainland?

BRIDGET. Well, as I say, I don't like to gossip. But the day before, she'd been seen with one of the supply ship workers. We mustn't be too quick to judge. There's little on an island like this for a young woman if she has certain ambitions.

ELSPETH. Had she any romantic alliances here on Skelthsea?

BRIDGET. ...Hettie made several 'conquests' in her time here. But you'll soon see the men here have little to offer a clever young woman. There's little to do but have children and work to fill their stomachs.

ELSPETH. Do you have children?

BRIDGET. No.

But I'm blessed. The congregation is a family. A sense of belonging. And *you* will find a sense of belonging here too, Elspeth.

But only if it's what you truly want. *(Connecting with* **ELSPETH**.*)* Some people run away to Skelthsea thinking they can leave whatever woes they amassed on the mainland far behind them.

ELSPETH. I'm not running from anything.

BRIDGET. You said something about grief...

ELSPETH. It was my sister. Clara. When she died, I couldn't see a life beyond my loss. Until finally, I accepted that my grief is incurable. It can't be mended like the broken stitches of a hem. And once I conceded that I would have to bear my silent shroud of grief for as long as I last, I found a freedom in it. It could no longer hold me, because I wasn't trying to escape it. And so I didn't come to Skelthsea to run from my loss but instead to see if there was a way I could use it, to offer help to someone who... *(Holding back tears.)*

*(**BRIDGET** puts a hand on **ELSPETH**.)*

BRIDGET. I think if anyone can help her, Elspeth, you can. You possess a warmth of character that someone like Mary needs.

ELSPETH. It's so strange. Sometimes a coincidence seems so unlikely that you think someone, somehow must have intervened.

BRIDGET. Coincidence?

ELSPETH. Miss Gillies told me of a fire at Iskar House years ago.

BRIDGET. Oh, yes.

ELSPETH. Despite the restoration, she said she still sees the house in its burnt-out state.

BRIDGET. What are you saying, Elspeth?

ELSPETH. *I* see so many places the same way. You see, Clara died in a house fire. And where someone else might see a roof, I see charred eaves. Where you see the windows, I see smashed and blackened panes. Where you see floorboards and rugs, I see the ash of everything I had loved.

> (**ELSPETH** *pulls herself together.*)

Bridget...what did your husband mean, in his sermon... about wickedness? Was he referring to William?

BRIDGET. There were rumours about William's fascination with the occult. Strange practices with animal bones and all sorts of unholy things. Let's just hope the poor boy is at peace now.

ELSPETH. What if he isn't?

BRIDGET. What do you mean?

ELSPETH. ...Sometimes, back at Iskar House, sometimes I hear...

I know it sounds silly but sometimes, at Iskar house, I hear a whistle.

BRIDGET. Someone whistling?

ELSPETH. No. A kind of airy, fife-like whistle. And suddenly, there's a chill...

BRIDGET. You know the wind through the cracks can...

ELSPETH. Yes. I know. I said it would sound silly.

I really should go. There's a doctor coming to the house to see Mary.

> (**MARY** *enters [in her own world]. She takes a seat and clutches Bobbity tightly.*)

BRIDGET. Is she unwell?

ELSPETH.   They're saying she might have to take up residency in some kind of, of institution, if she makes no improvement.

BRIDGET.   But she's a grieving child.

ELSPETH.   That's why I want to be there. I'm sure Miss Gillies wants the best for Mary but I'm not sure she always knows what that is.

> *(They exit separately, and we are suddenly into the next scene.)*

Scene Seven

(**MARY** *sits on a chair. She holds Bobbity.*
A **DOCTOR** *has his stethoscope on Bobbity's*
chest.)

DOCTOR. Well, I'm afraid Bobbity's heart is a little weaker than I would like. As for you, Mary, you're in the best of health.

MISS GILLIES. She still isn't speaking, Doctor.

DOCTOR. I can see that.

It's been how long since William died?

MISS GILLIES. *(Abruptly.)* U-hm. We don't think it helps Mary to keep dwelling on her brother.

DOCTOR. No matter how much you avoid the subject, Miss Gillies, the fact won't change.

Mary, is there anything in particular that troubles you?

(**ELSPETH** *bursts in.)*

ELSPETH. I'm sorry I'm late –

MISS GILLIES. You don't need to be here, Elspeth.

DOCTOR. Who is this…?

ELSPETH. I'm the girl's nanny.

DOCTOR. Ah, then it might be useful if you did stay.

(To **GREER**.*)* I thought you were the nanny?

GREER. *(Pointedly.)* I'm just the housemaid.

DOCTOR. Oh, then… We don't need too many people.

(Awkward moment.)

MISS GILLIES. Thank you, Greer.

(**GREER** *gives the impression of exiting but instead takes up her broom and sweeps within the vicinity. Listening.*)

DOCTOR. Mary, you haven't spoken since your brother died. Do you *hope* to speak again?

ELSPETH. I don't think forcing her is –

MISS GILLIES. Elspeth!

(*Beat.*)

DOCTOR. And tell me, Miss…?

ELSPETH. Swansome.

DOCTOR. Miss Swansome, has Mary shown signs of speaking to you?

ELSPETH. I haven't attempted to make her speak.

(**GREER** *sighs exasperatedly. She hasn't even been trying!*)

I imagine she will speak when she so chooses. When she is ready.

DOCTOR. (*To* **MARY**.) And what about laughter? Do you laugh?

(**MARY** *nods.*)

(**DOCTOR** *looks to* **ELSPETH**.)

ELSPETH. Yes, when we play.

DOCTOR. And what about singing?

MARY. …

(**DOCTOR** *looks to* **MISS GILLIES**…)

MISS GILLIES. No, she doesn't sing.

ELSPETH. I wonder…

(All eyes on **ELSPETH***.)*

ELSPETH.   I wonder if sometimes... you see, Doctor, Mary occasionally sleepwalks. Isn't that right? And sometimes, sometimes in the night I hear someone singing a child's lullaby.

GREER. *(Suddenly back in the scene.)* I haven't heard it and I'm an especially light sleeper.

(All eyes on **GREER***. They thought she had left.)*

*(***GREER** *goes back to her sweeping. Still listening.)*

ELSPETH. I wondered if it was Greer –

GREER. What, serenading you?

ELSPETH. But, perhaps in her sleep, Mary –

MISS GILLIES. I don't think speculaton is helping.

ELSPETH. I'm just trying to help the doctor.

DOCTOR. Very well. Thank you. Both of you. *(To* **GREER***.)* All three of you.

Mary, when you sleepwalk, do you recall what happened in the morning?

*(***MARY** *shakes her head, no.)*

ELSPETH. You can see, she's perfectly able to communicate. And the other day, down on the beach she was able to write in the sand. We were looking at the birds –

DOCTOR. All right, all right. I think what we all want is the bcst for Mary. We may differ in our view as to what that is and how to achieve it. It's my feeling that we give Mary another few weeks before I assess her again. But we can't wait in vain hope indefinitely.

(*To* **MISS GILLIES**.) If she has made no real progress by my return, then I think the best thing would be to have her cared for in an institution that is equipped for –

ELSPETH. No!

GREER. Miss Swansome!

MISS GILLIES. Thank you, Greer. That'll be all…

> (**GREER** *exits.*)

ELSPETH. I need time. I've barely started. Already, I feel there are improvements.

DOCTOR. Then you put it on your own shoulders, Miss Swansome. A month, and then we need to take action.

Thank you, Miss Gillies.

> (**MISS GILLIES** *shows the* **DOCTOR** *out.*)

> (**MARY** *and* **ELSPETH** *alone.* **ELSPETH** *takes* **MARY**'s *hand.*)

ELSPETH. Don't worry, Mary. I won't let them take you away.

> (**MARY** *cries.* **ELSPETH** *comforts her.*)

Oh, come here.

After Clara died, I too retreated to a place beyond the reach of others. There's nothing wrong with you, Mary. But if there is something particular that's troubling you, I'm not asking you to speak, but please, please try to find a way to tell me, so I can help…

> (**MARY** *looks as if she has something to say.*)

Is there something?

> (**MARY** *looks* **ELSPETH** *in the eye.*)

(*Urgently; she is onto something.*) Is it about William?

(**MARY** *clenches her mouth shut.*)

(Urgently.) Or Hettie?

(**MARY** *wants to say something but her better judgement won't permit it.*)

Mary, what –

(Suddenly, purposefully, **MISS GILLIES** *comes in.)*

MISS GILLIES. Mary, go and play in your room, please.

(**MARY** *exits.*)

Elspeth, I have opened my home to you, but you must know your place.

ELSPETH. You told me that my place was to help Mary. How will she ever speak if the one thing she might want to talk about is forbidden?

MISS GILLIES. You don't understand. William had... William was not well, in his mind... it is better for her not to dwell on it. If you don't like how we do things here, you can do as Hettie did.

(**MISS GILLIES** *exits.*)

(**ELSPETH** *remains.*)

(Darkness begins to fall.)

Scene Eight

*(Music takes us into **ELSPETH**'s mind. She takes her locket.)*

*(The curtain in **ELSPETH**'s room billows in the wind. Darkness outside. **ELSPETH** shuts the window. The sound of a whistle. Chilling. **ELSPETH** startled.)*

ELSPETH. It isn't just the wind...

(Silence.)

*(**ELSPETH** begins preparing herself for bed.)*

(The lullaby is sung from somewhere.)

Mary. Is that –

*(**ELSPETH** silences herself. Decides to try to catch the lullaby singer. **HOUSE SHADOWS** enter. Music, lullaby, movement all interacting.)*

*(The lullaby continues. It is distant. It fades and resumes. It appears to be coming from one place and then another. It's almost enough to make **ELSPETH** lose her bearings.)*

(She continues to look. Nothing.)

(She gets to the door for William's wing. It's ajar. She stops.)

It's supposed to be locked?

*(**ELSPETH** checks no one is watching. She exits through the door.)*

(**HOUSE SHADOWS** *float dusty/mouldering white sheets over all furniture.*)

(**HOUSE SHADOWS** *cover themselves in their own floating costumes and fall still. They have become the sheeted furniture of William's wing.*)

(*Large toy soldiers on a shelf.*)

(*A new darkness.*)

(**ELSPETH** *enters from a new doorway.*)

(*She lights some candles, but it's barely enough.*)

(*She moves around the sheeted furniture.*)

(*A toy soldier falls. Slight shock.* **ELSPETH** *replaces it.*)

Mary? You're not supposed to be in here. William's wing is –

(*Suddenly, a window bangs open. Loud.*)

(*The pages of an open book fan noisily.*)

(*Then a sound.*)

(*A clockwork fire truck enters.*)

(*Behind her, unseen to* **ELSPETH**, *a figure, draped in black enters. The figure watches* **ELSPETH**.)

(*The figure is singing the lullaby – we still can't see who it is.*)

(**ELSPETH** *turns.*)

(But the figure stops still. **ELSPETH** *sees nothing.)*

(Floorboards creak as **ELSPETH** *moves.)*

(The figure whisper-sings the lullaby.)

(Quite scared now.) Mary? If you come out, I could sing with you if you –

*(***ELSPETH*** *sees a small wooden chest. Intrigued. She opens it. Furtively, checking no one is watching,* **ELSPETH** *takes out a bag. She unfastens the bag and takes out some strange items.)*

(All **HOUSE SHADOWS** *look up at what* **ELSPETH** *has found.)*

(A bird skeleton. A stone wrapped in hair. A sheep's skull. A bone whistle. The findings horrify **ELSPETH.***)*

(She hurriedly places the items back in the bag, back into the chest, puts the chest back. As she does this, we see the dark figure has crept up behind **ELSPETH***. Right behind her.)*

*(***ELSPETH*** *feels a presence. Turns. No one there.)*

(A noise from somewhere elsc.)

*(***ELSPETH*** *looks.)*

*(***MARY*** *enters, holding Bobbity. She is sleepwalking. Otherworldly. Whispering to herself. No words are formed or comprehensible.)*

Mary…!

(But **MARY** *is still in her own world.)*

Mary, are you all right?

*(***MARY*** continues to walk as if she cannot hear, completely unaware of* **ELSPETH***'s presence.)*

Can you hear me? It's Elspeth.

*(***ELSPETH*** shakes* **MARY** *by the shoulders.)*

Mary, wake up! Wake up!

*(***MARY*** comes around.)*

You were sleepwalking again.

MARY. ...

ELSPETH. That's all right. I just don't want you to have an accident. Your aunt is right, it's dangerous here.

(She hugs **MARY***.)*

I think you were singing. A lullaby. In your sleep. It's lovely to hear your voice. We can sing together if you like.

MARY. ...

ELSPETH. *(Sings.)*
I WALK WITH MY LITTLE LANTERN / MY LANTERN MYSELF AND I...

(But **MARY** *has seen something over* **ELSPETH***'s shoulder.)*

(The **HOUSE SHADOWS***, dreamlike, slowly disrobe the dark figure to reveal a deathly young woman – tortured dress, lank hair, a large needle through her nose.)*

IN HEAVEN THE STARS ARE SHINING / DOWN HERE WE'RE STARS TO THE SKY.

(**ELSPETH** *interrupts herself.*)

What is it, Mary?

(**MARY** *continues to look beyond* **ELSPETH**.)

(*The young woman puts her finger to her lips for silence.*)

(**ELSPETH** *turns.*)

(*Quickly,* **HOUSE SHADOWS** *cover the figure in their flowing costumes.*)

(*Sheeted furniture and silence.*)

Come along. There's a terrible chill. Let's get you back to bed.

(**ELSPETH** *extinguishes candles.*)

(*They begin to exit.* **ELSPETH** *thinks for a moment. She goes back and takes the bag of William's weird items from the chest.*)

(*Music.*)

(**HOUSE SHADOWS** *exit.*)

(**ELSPETH** *exits.*)

(**GREER** *enters. Furtive. She opens William's small chest and sees the bag of items has been taken.*)

GREER. Elspeth... Interfering little...

(*Angrily,* **GREER** *exits.*)

(*Suddenly, morning light.*)

(*Seagulls scream.*)

Scene Nine

*(**AILSA***'s cottage. Dead fish, Game, seaweed hang from the ceiling.)*

*(**AILSA** stands alone. She is preparing sheep's wool for the loom with sharp metal tools.)*

*(She suddenly sees something. She momentarily exits; returns with **ELSPETH**.)*

AILSA. You don't have Mary with you.

ELSPETH. No.

AILSA. I didn't think you'd bring her.

ELSPETH. But you knew I would come?

AILSA. I *told* you you would come.

(Pointing to the seaweed.) Seaweed, you see...

Boil its goodness into a stew, into my medicines. The rest goes on the vegetable patches.

Let me pour you some of this.

*(She pours **ELSPETH** a green drink. **ELSPETH** recoils at the sight of it.)*

Take a seat; you don't have to stand on ceremony. You're not at Iskar House now.

*(**ELSPETH** does not take a seat.)*

ELSPETH. Ailsa, when Mary and I met you on the beach the other day, you said that all is not well at Iskar House. What did you mean by that?

AILSA. Do you really need to ask?

ELSPETH. ...?

AILSA. Are you not learning the ways of those in Iskar? Miss Violet Gillies. Greer. I'm sure you could tell me more of their peculiarities than I can tell you.

ELSPETH. I wouldn't want to be disloyal.

AILSA. No need for airs here, Miss Swansome. You don't want to be disloyal – did you tell Miss Gillies you were coming here?

ELSPETH. …

AILSA. Of course not. You don't want to be found consorting with the outcast witch of Skelthsea.

ELSPETH. Are you truly outcast?

AILSA. Aren't you? Escaping to a remote island. Cast out from your privileged situation.

ELSPETH. That's not how it is.

AILSA. But you come from privilege. It's in every word you speak.

ELSPETH. Even those from privilege can suffer the same grief as those who do not. When my parents passed away, my sister and I… we had nothing.

AILSA. And then you run away to a family in mourning. Maybe you seek grief.

ELSPETH. Or maybe it seeks me. I never even knew William and yet I find myself sharing the anguish caused by his accident.

AILSA. *(Dismissively.)* Psh…

ELSPETH. You disagree?

AILSA. I believe William's death caused anguish. What I don't believe is that it was caused by an accident.

ELSPETH. What?!

AILSA. *(Grabbing* **ELSPETH***'s wrist.)* William's death. It was no accident.

ELSPETH. But he was found below Stack Mor. He slipped and –

AILSA. Do you know my role on the island, Miss Swansome?

ELSPETH. No.

AILSA. I assist the dead.

ELSPETH. Assist the –?

AILSA. Oh, the people of Skelthsea have pushed me out of polite circles, out of the church. But the Reverend Argyle has no trouble calling on me to do the work he can't face.

ELSPETH. How do you mean?

AILSA. I cleanse the bodies ready for burial. I dress them. I place the coin on the tongue. Sew the eyes and the mouth closed ready for them to meet whoever they believe their maker might be.

ELSPETH. What has that to do with William?

AILSA. Because I tended to him after his death. "Poor, poor William," they say. "Fell from Stack Mor," they say. "A terrible accident," they…

I saw the wounds that child bore. And they were many, believe you me. But he didn't bleed the way he should. His heart had stopped a-thumping long before he fell from that cliff.

ELSPETH. What are you trying to say?

AILSA. I'm saying, Miss Swansome, somebody killed that boy and threw him down Stack Mor. And you know what that means…?

ELSPETH. …That somebody on this island is a murderer.

> (**AILSA** *takes her long smoking pipe and twists tobacco into it. Lights it and smokes throughout the following…*)

No. No, why would someone want to kill a young boy?

AILSA. You have no ideas of your own?

> (**AILSA** *searches* **ELSPETH***'s eyes.*)

You've not heard rumours?

Nobody at Iskar House whispering about William's descent into darkness?

> (*Beat.*)

> (**ELSPETH** *offers the bag taken from William's wing.*)

What's this?

ELSPETH. I found these in William's room. Miss Gillies won't let anyone go in there but –

AILSA. But you knew something was wrong.

> (**AILSA** *takes the items out of the bag. The stone wrapped in hair.*)

ELSPETH. I found another stone like this in Hettie's room.

AILSA. A stone wrapped in hair. It's binding magic. It's to tie one person to another for eternity. Or, sometimes in witchcraft, to bind a person to sickness, or to death.

> (**AILSA** *takes out the bird skeleton and sheep's skull.*)

Animal sacrifice. Common in paganism, of course. Not to mention witchcraft.

And – (*Gasps.*)

> (*Taking the next item from the back. The bone whistle.*)

(*Concerned.*) Have you blown this?!

ELSPETH. No, I –

AILSA. Then don't!

ELSPETH. What is it?

AILSA. This is a widow's whistle. Made from bone – sometimes human. A widow would blow it to raise the spirit of her deceased husband.

ELSPETH. Why would William keep such an object?

AILSA. It seems as if he practised rituals to consort with the dead. Some souls are made to be dark. The world gives birth to both the viper and the lamb. Our job is to distinguish between the two.

That's why Miss Gillies won't talk to you about William; the idea that he was caught up in a darkness she finds so abhorrent.

ELSPETH. The whistle…

AILSA. Yes?

ELSPETH. Oh, I'm not sure…

> (**AILSA** *waits, smoking.*)

There are times when I have heard a whistle being blown.

AILSA. This whistle?

ELSPETH. I don't know. I found this in William's wing. It would seem strange that someone should go there just to blow the whistle.

AILSA. But you've heard it. And has there been anything… unusual?

ELSPETH. I don't believe in the supernatural… But there are some things I can't explain. I sometimes wonder if Mary feels it too. Oh! I need to get back for her now, her lessons will be finishing.

What should I do with all these?

AILSA. You should put them back where you found them. They were not yours to disturb. The more human hands touch these items, the more they connect to the world beyond.

>(**ELSPETH** *puts the items back in the bag, leaves.*)

>(*Suddenly, seagulls scream shrilly.*)

Scene Ten

(Seagulls still scream. Waves against rocks.)

*(**ISLANDERS** enter in coats and hats. They gather at the sealine.)*

*(Two **ISLANDERS** drag a human body-shaped package up onto the island [stage].)*

ISLANDER 3. That's it. Don't let the water drag it back.

ISLANDER 4. Stand back a pace, will you.

*(The **ISLANDERS** all step back. They can see what it is. Shock. Gasps. Some cover their mouths in horror.)*

(We see what they see: a body wrapped in sail cloth. A decomposing arm/hand sticks out from the wrappings.)

ISLANDER 1. Looks like a sea burial.

ISLANDER 2. The body must have come loose from its weights and drifted in on the storm.

*(**ELSPETH** and **MARY** enter.)*

*(**MARY** goes to see.)*

ELSPETH. What's happening?

Mary, don't get too close.

*(**ELSPETH** sees what it is. Stops.)*

Mary, don't look.

*(**MARY** sees it, also, and retreats to **ELSPETH** for comfort.)*

ISLANDER 3. Could have been a passenger on one of the steam ships. That would be my guess.

*(An **ISLANDER** kneels down and opens the wrappings.)*

(Everyone aghast.)

ISLANDER 2. Who is it?

ISLANDER 1. A woman, I think.

*(**MARY** tugs at **ELSPETH**'s arm.)*

ELSPETH. What, Mary?

*(**MARY** points to the body.)*

What do you see?

*(**MARY** points.)*

*(The **ISLANDERS** now see that **MARY** knows something.)*

ISLANDER 1. Is it someone you know?

MARY. …

ISLANDER 4. *(Impatiently.)* Just tell us out loud, girl.

ISLANDER 3. Just speak, child, if you know something.

*(**MARY** intimidated by the **ISLANDERS**, but points again – specifically.*

ISLANDER 1. Is it this? *(Unpinning a brooch.)* It's a brooch.

ELSPETH. Do you know who it belongs to?

ISLANDER 2. Who is it?

*(**MARY**, still intimidated by the crowd, but writes in the sand for **ELSPETH** to see.)*

ELSPETH. "Hettie."

She's saying the brooch belongs to Hettie.

(Seagulls scream. Blackout.)

ACT TWO

Scene One

(Gulls Cry Cottage. An abandoned cottage, taken over by dust, mice and damp. A bucket catches water from a leak. Audible drips.)

(Drip.)

BOY'S VOICE. Drip.

(Drip.)

Drip.

(Drip.)

Drip.

(The **VOICE** *stops but the drips continue throughout.)*

*(***ELSPETH** *and* **MARY** *enter.* **MARY** *leads* **ELSPETH** *by the hand.)*

ELSPETH. Are you sure no one will mind us being in here?

Whose cottage is this?

*(***MARY** *goes to a drawer/cupboard and gets out an album. Shows it to* **ELSPETH**.*)*

Gulls Cry Cottage. The cottage is owned by your family?

(**MARY** *nods.*)

This is you. And is that...is that William?

(**MARY** *nods.*)

(*Still looking at the picture.*) Goodness. You look so alike. You could almost be...

You were twins?

(**MARY** *nods.*)

I didn't know...

Oh, Mary.

And is that your mother?

(**MARY** *nods.*)

But you didn't live here? I thought you always lived at Iskar House?

(**MARY** *points to a picture of* **MISS GILLIES**.)

Miss Gillies. Your aunt lived here.

(**MARY** *nods.*)

And then she moved in with you at Iskar after your mother's passing?

(**MARY** *nods.*)

(*She takes the album to an area that's set up. Cushion/blanket. A few dolls. This is her secret little place.*)

Do you often come here?

(**MARY** *nods. She sets Bobbity with the dolls.*)

(**MARY** *continues to look through the photo album.*)

You come here...you come here to be close to William?

(**MARY** *nods.*)

I do feel for you.

To find ways of keeping close to those we've lost is difficult enough, without having to do it in secrecy.

I don't have many pictures of my sister, Clara.

She was younger than me. She wasn't always well... I used to care for her. She died last year. I still ask myself how does one continue when the person you love the most is gone.

(**MARY** *nods in agreement/understanding.*)

I think you're the only person I've met who truly knows what it is to lose a brother or sister.

I keep this one with me though. Always. She's always with me.

(*Shows* **MARY** *the picture.*)

(**MARY** *puts a hand on* **ELSPETH**'s *to comfort her.*)

Thank you.

(*Tentatively, they are closer.* **MARY** *suddenly disquieted. She wants to tell* **ELSPETH** *something but she can't.*)

What is it, Mary? You brought me here, to your secret place, to tell me something, didn't you?

(**MARY** *takes a large Bible from the detritus. Opens it.*)

(**ELSPETH** *thinks this might be a game.*)

(**MARY** *points to a letter on the page.*)

"I"

> (**MARY** *finds another place on the page and points.*)

"am"

> (**MARY** *turns the pages until she finds the next word. Points.*)

"Going"

(Smiling.) Where are you going?

> (**MARY** *repeats the action, finding the next word.*)

"to"

Going to where?

> (**MARY** *repeats the action. Finds the word.* **ELSPETH** *shocked. We should feel it.*)

Mary, why on earth would you say that?! Why did you say you're going to die? Has someone threatened –

> *(Loud bang.)*

> *(Suddenly a case falls off a shelf.)*

Who's there?

> (**ELSPETH** *gets up to look.*)

> (**MARY** *goes and sits next to the bucket. She watches the drips fall. Enjoying the rhythm of it. Faintly, we hear the* **BOY'S VOICE**: *Drip, drip…*)

(Trying to convince herself.) We must have knocked it when we came through.

> (**ELSPETH** *picks the case up, but it falls open.*)

*(**ELSPETH** looks in the case and takes out a couple of newly-knitted baby clothes. Holds them up to show **MARY**.)*

These baby clothes would almost fit Bobbity.

(In the case is a purse. She opens it.)

(To herself.) Strange to leave money lying around like this... Do you –

(But she changes her mind when she sees something in the purse. Music/atmosphere should indicate the significance.)

*(**MARY** looks up. **ELSPETH** hides the purse behind her own back.)*

Mary, thank you for sharing your special place with me. If Miss Gillies doesn't mind, maybe we could bring some oil next time and light some lamps.

*(Without warning, **GREER** has entered.)*

GREER. Miss Gillies *does* mind.

You know you're not supposed to be in here, Mary.

ELSPETH. *(Still concealing the purse.)* Then how did you know where to find her?

GREER. There are no hiding places on Skelthsea.

ELSPETH. Evidently. And why did you need to come looking?

GREER. The Reverend Argyle's having tea at the house. He came by to see Mary.

ELSPETH. Why?

GREER. That's a matter for him and Mary. Come on.

*(**MARY** goes to **GREER** and together they exit. A shared look between **MARY** and **ELSPETH**.)*

(**ELSPETH** *watches as* **GREER** *takes* **MARY** *away.*)

(**ELSPETH** *inspects the purse again. Deeply concerned by what she has found.*)

Scene Two

(The sound of rain. **HETTIE***'s funeral.)*

(The entire cast huddle with umbrellas and coats.)

(A hymn is sung.)

ROBERT. And while we all knew so little of this young woman, we took her onto our island and into our hearts. And now, whatever sins she might have committed, it is the duty of all of us to give her our prayers as she makes her journey into the hands of our Lord. From dust we came, to dust we return.

(The mourners disperse.)

(As **ELSPETH** *turns away,* **BRIDGET** *joins her. Holds an umbrella over her.)*

BRIDGET. You seem so troubled by all of this, Elspeth.

ELSPETH. I'm concerned.

BRIDGET. Hettie's fate isn't your fate.

ELSPETH. I'm concerned for Mary.

BRIDGET. Yes. Robert's been worried about the effect it would have on her – seeing the body of Hettie. He's a grown man and the effect of finding the body of little William stays with him. That's why he called round to see Mary yesterday.

ELSPETH. I think she has seen so much death that she expects it is coming to her.

BRIDGET. She has been through a lot, the poor lamb. She still hasn't been able to speak at all?

ELSPETH. She's finding her own ways to communicate with me. She took me to the cottage where Miss Gillies used to live.

BRIDGET. Gulls Cry cottage?

ELSPETH. Yes.

BRIDGET. Miss Gillies needs to light a fire in there once in a while to keep the damp away.

ELSPETH. So, Miss Gillies lived there until the children's mother died?

BRIDGET. That's right. Evangeline, William and Mary always lived in Iskar House. When Evangeline died, William legally inherited it. Violet left Gull's Cry Cottage and moved to Iskar House to look after them.

ELSPETH. So, Miss Gillies doesn't... I was under the impression that she owned the house.

BRIDGET. No. She certainly does not.

ELSPETH. Oh. Is it a point of contention?

BRIDGET. I was close to Evangeline. And...well, you know I'm not one for gossip, but there was bad blood between Violet and Evangeline Gillies. Their father left the big house to Evangeline and Gulls Cry Cottage to Violet. Violet felt pushed out of her own home.

ELSPETH. But William's dead now. Who –

BRIDGET. Mary. Evangeline made it so that Mary inherited Iskar House in the unlikely event of William passing. Miss Gillies is only living there until Mary is of age.

ELSPETH. So, if Mary died... If Mary died, who –

BRIDGET. Miss Gillies is the only other living relative. She would inherit.

ELSPETH. Was Miss Gillies close to the children before their mother passed away?

BRIDGET. ...Some women never want children, while some of us are never blessed with them.

ELSPETH. I'm sorry. You dearly wanted children of your own, didn't you?

BRIDGET. Robert as much as I. I carried three, you know.

ELSPETH. Oh, Bridget.

BRIDGET. It's all right. In the end, we had to let it go...

(Smiling stoically.) You have a comforting manner, Elspeth. I've never spoken of my losses before.

ELSPETH. Well, I hope I can ease your burden if in any way at all.

BRIDGET. I think you've enough burden of your own. Don't let the troubles at Iskar House become your own troubles.

ELSPETH. ...Bridget, I... At the cottage, Mary wanted to show me pictures of William. You know there isn't a single picture of William at Iskar House.

*(**ELSPETH** checks no one is watching them.)*

Bridget, while I was there, I found...

Maybe I shouldn't have looked, but...

BRIDGET. What did you find?

*(**ELSPETH** takes out the purse.)*

ELSPETH. I found this purse.

(She opens the purse. Takes out a picture.)

This picture is of Hettie and the two children, isn't it?

BRIDGET. Yes, that's Hettie.

ELSPETH. And look at this. This is a lot of money to someone like Hettie. And this. This dolphin pendant. These were all in a case. Like she was set to leave.

BRIDGET. She did leave.

ELSPETH. But why would she leave without taking what must have been her most valuable possessions?

BRIDGET. What are you saying, Elspeth?

ELSPETH. Was there anyone who might have wanted her gone?

You said she had dalliances on the island...

BRIDGET. All I heard were rumours...hearsay.

ELSPETH. I thought there are no secrets on Skelthsea. Who was Hettie intimate with?

BRIDGET. ...Have you met the chap who owns the shop?

ELSPETH. Paterson? But he's so...repellent. Surely Hettie wouldn't have been foolish enough to...

BRIDGET. People get lonely here. Perhaps he knows how to flatter a woman, to make her feel as if she matters.

Look, I wouldn't read too much into these rumours. People do love to gossip. That doesn't mean it's true

ELSPETH. But what if Hettie didn't die at sea? What if she died here?

BRIDGET. Elspeth –

ELSPETH. Your husband must have seen the body before burial. Did he say if there was anything...unusual.

BRIDGET. He doesn't prepare the bodies. That's –

ELSPETH. Ailsa.

> *(Suddenly, dead fish, game and seaweed hanging from hooks appear and we are with **AILSA** in her kitchen.)*

AILSA. I cleansed that girl's body. I cleaned it with soap and I cleansed her soul with supplications. Whatever she might have been entangled with in life, she's all square with her maker now.

ELSPETH. What do you mean?

AILSA. It was Hettie that taught William the ways of the pagan, the ways of darkness. That's what they say, anyway.

ELSPETH. Do you believe that?

AILSA. On Skelthsea, it's difficult to know where rumours end and the truth begins.

ELSPETH. Is it certain that Hettie died at sea?

(**AILSA** *fills and lights her pipe.*)

AILSA. You know the tradition of sea burials is to stitch sail cloth around the body and then push the needle through the nose of the deceased.

Make sure the person's really dead. (*Enacting it!*)

ELSPETH. And had the needle gone through her nose?

AILSA. Aye.

ELSPETH. But it was you who told me there was a murderer on this island.

AILSA. I told you William died before he fell. But I can't speak for Hettie. It looked like a sea burial to me.

ELSPETH. Ailsa. You told me about the widow's whistle, of the hair-bound stones and how they call to the dead. Do you believe that such objects can achieve their purpose?

AILSA. Why do you ask?

ELSPETH. You know why I ask, don't you? You told me all is not well at Iskar House. You know it is full of things that do not make sense – at least in the world I understand.

AILSA. People say that those who *believe* in life beyond the grave are mad, or witches. Oh, they have the worst of all possible names for us. But off they all go to *their* church, singing to *their* god, performing *their* rituals and sacrifices.

All we can know is what we see and feel for ourselves. Whose judgement do you trust?

ELSPETH. All the beliefs I have spent my life in certainty of no longer seem adequate. I see... I hear...impossible things.

AILSA. Then you have your answer.

ELSPETH. There's no one at the house I can speak to. Miss Gillies is secretive... And Greer. I don't know why she must be the way she is with me.

AILSA. She was the same with Hettie. You know why, surely?

ELSPETH. Why?

AILSA. She wanted your job. She wanted the job of nannying those two unfortunate souls. Greer wants you out of the way, so she makes you feel uncomfortable. Believe me, I know Greer better than most on this island.

She knows, does Greer – she knows the dead can return. She's sought my advice on this over the years. Trying to contact her poor old mother. Has anyone told you about her?

ELSPETH. No.

AILSA. Greer's mother worked at Iskar House. She had an accident. Fell from an upstairs window and died. Greer remained and grew up in Iskar House alongside the Gillies sisters. Evangeline and Violet. The two young mistresses of the house and poor wee Greer. That's why Violet would never allow Greer to be the nanny. She could never see her as more than a housemaid's daughter.

ELSPETH. So Greer has suffered at Iskar House.

I think somebody at the house means harm to me, and to Mary too.

AILSA. Then you need to be careful.

> (**ELSPETH** *turns to leave.* **AILSA** *grabs her wrist.*)

If you decide the spirits are real, there are ways to banish them – if you trust me.

> (**AILSA** *exits.*)

Scene Three

(Iskar House. Daylight.)

*(**MARY** enters with an easel.)*

ELSPETH. If you're going to draw me, then I think it's only
fair that I should draw you.

> *(**ELSPETH** takes a drawing board and paper.
> She stands to draw **MARY** as **MARY** stands at
> the easel to draw **ELSPETH**.)*

(Playfully.) Now, let me look at those ears. Yes, they're
very much like a cat's ears. I shall certainly make
something of those.

> *(**MARY** laughs. But restrains herself.)*

> *(**ELSPETH** continues.)*

Now, do I include Bobbity in this picture or is Bobbity
off having an adventure?

> *(**MARY** holds Bobbity tightly.)*

I see.

> *(As **MARY** tries to draw, **ELSPETH** hides her
> own face behind the drawing board. A kind of
> peek-a-boo. It amuses **MARY**.)*

My sister was always a good drawer. She liked to draw
the busy streets of Edinburgh. Have you ever been to
the mainland?

> *(**MARY** shakes her head, no.)*

I would love to show you the market. Full of the smells
of cakes, and cooking meat, and stalls of flowers of
every colour, and jewellery that sparkles in the sunlight.

(**MARY** *then writes a note on her paper and tears it off. She hands it to* **ELSPETH**.)

"I will miss you"

No. I told you, I'm not going to let them take you away.

(**MARY** *shakes her head, no. She points to* **ELSPETH**.)

Me? *I'm* going away?

(**MARY** *nods.*)

Mary, I'm not going anywhere. Where do you think I'm going?

(**PATERSON** *enters, unexpectedly.*)

Mr Paterson...

PATERSON. I did try the bell. The door was ajar, so I...

ELSPETH. What can we do for you?

PATERSON. I just came by with these sweets for Mary.

(*But he holds them out for* **ELSPETH** *to take.*)

I know it's been a difficult time for her. We have to pull together here on Skelthsea. Look out for one another.

(**ELSPETH** *does not take the gift.*)

ELSPETH. Mary, look. A gift. For you.

(**MARY** *tries for a smile.* **ELSPETH** *gestures to* **MARY**. **MARY** *holds out her hand.* **PATERSON** *hands them to* **MARY**.)

PATERSON. I know that you like these ones.

(**MARY** *doesn't react.*)

ELSPETH. Thank you.

PATERSON. And what about you?

ELSPETH. ...?

PATERSON. What do you like?

ELSPETH. I have everything I need, thank you.

PATERSON. I haven't seen you at my shop. Has the mistress warned you away from me?

ELSPETH. I have had no need of any purchases.

PATERSON. Oh, that can't be –

ELSPETH. There can be no other reason to visit a shop unless I need something.

PATERSON. It must have been difficult for you, too. Your predecessor ending up the way she did.

ELSPETH. Hettie's death is difficult for everyone here.

Perhaps for you too. You knew her well, I'm told?

PATERSON. *(Caught off guard.)* ...Not really. A little, maybe.

ELSPETH. You miss her?

PATERSON. I hardly knew her.

You must wonder what you have walked into, Miss Swansome. It isn't usually like this here.

ELSPETH. What is it usually like?

PATERSON. Skelthsea is the kind of the place where you are woken every morning by the sound of the waves against shingle, the gulls' cry on the breeze. And as the sun slips through the gap in your curtains, you... *(Shy.)* oh, well, maybe I romanticise too much.

> *(She softens.)*

Does Miss Gillies ever let you take the evening off?

(He approaches **ELSPETH**.*)*

I could take you for a drink.

ELSPETH. I don't drink.

PATERSON. I could take you dancing.

ELSPETH. There's nowhere to dance on Skelthsea.

PATERSON. Then we could dance here.

> *(***PATERSON*** takes* **ELSPETH***'s hand and forces her into a dance.)*

ELSPETH. No! I –

> *(***ELSPETH*** trips and* **PATERSON*** grabs her.)*

> *(***GREER*** and* **MISS GILLIES*** enter.)*

MISS GILLIES. Miss Swansome!

PATERSON. Ah, I'm sure this looks worse than it is.

ELSPETH. *(Straightening her clothes.)* Mr Paterson came to give Mary some sweets.

MISS GILLIES. *(Sarcastic.)* Isn't he thoughtful?

Greer. Could you see Mr Paterson is able to find his way out?

(Regarding the easel.) And what have you been doing, Mary?

ELSPETH. She wanted to draw me.

> *(***MISS GILLIES*** look at* **MARY***'s easel. She sighs, exasperated.)*

What's wrong?

> *(***ELSPETH*** looks at the easel.)*

MISS GILLIES. Was it your idea that she draw her brother?

ELSPETH. No, but –

MISS GILLIES. Mary, take the rest of your things to your room.

(**MARY** *takes the drawing and exits.*)

ELSPETH. Can't she express her love and her grief for William? Living here where there is no mention, no sign of William having ever lived, it makes it difficult for her.

MISS GILLIES. I understand that you and Mary went to Gull's Cry Cottage.

ELSPETH. No... Mary wanted to show me it. I gather it was your home.

MISS GILLIES. Once.

ELSPETH. You don't ever wish to return?

MISS GILLIES. Iskar is my home.

It is clear to me that we can't go on like this. Mary continues to sleepwalk, to dream herself awake. And whatever your interest in Paterson may be, it's beneath the dignity of Iskar House. I appreciate you've tried your best, Elspeth, I do, but she is showing no signs of speaking.

ELSPETH. I am certain she is making progress. Miss Gillies, I can –

MISS GILLIES. No. I've made up my mind. It's too late to send her on tomorrow's boat, but I will send a letter to the mainland that Mary is to take a place in the doctor's care.

I hope the two of you can continue together in the meantime.

(**MISS GILLIES** *exits.*)

Scene Four

(The onset of evening.)

(ELSPETH *enters her bedroom to find* **GREER** *in there, packing* **ELSPETH***'s things into a suitcase.)*

ELSPETH. Greer! What are you –

GREER. There's a boat in the morning. I thought I'd help you on your way.

ELSPETH. I'm not leaving Mary.

GREER. Mary will be leaving herself soon. You don't belong here.

ELSPETH. I can still help her.

*(***GREER** *squares up to* **ELSPETH***.)*

GREER. I know it was you.

ELSPETH. What?

GREER. You have taken the key to William's Wing.

ELSPETH. I have never seen a key to William's Wing.

GREER. Then how did you get in there?

ELSPETH. The door was... how do you know I went in there?

GREER. ...You have been told by Miss Gillies that William's Wing is out of bounds.

ELSPETH. I went to William's Wing because I could hear noises coming from there. I thought Mary was sleepwalking. Everything I have done since coming to Iskar House has been solely for the care of Mary.

GREER. And now it's time you left.

ELSPETH. I told you. I will not leave Mary.

GREER. Can't you see you have done her more harm than good?

ELSPETH. That's not –

GREER. Miss Gillies was doing everything she could to prevent Mary going off to that asylum. Since you've been here Mary has gone backwards. Encouraging her to think about William and death rather than getting better.

ELSPETH. How can she ever hope to find peace if she can't learn to live with her loss?

GREER. You are bringing her nothing but sorrow. Since the day you arrived, you've burdened Mary with your own grief.

ELSPETH. That was never my intention. I –

GREER. If you really cared for Mary, you would do what's best for her and leave on tomorrow's boat!

> (*Beat.*)

If you have the key to William's Wing, return it before you leave.

> (**GREER** *exits.*)

> (*Music. Sad.* **ELSPETH** *looks at the case. Tries to work out what to do. She begins to unpack. She takes out an item of clothing –*)

> (*Suddenly,* **MISS GILLIES** *appears. It should make* **ELSPETH** *and us jump.*)

MISS GILLIES. Elspeth, I've written to the doctor and – Oh. You're packing...

ELSPETH. No, I – (*Still holding the item of clothing.*)

MISS GILLIES. No, perhaps you're right. Perhaps it would be for the best.

ELSPETH. No, really –

MISS GILLIES. It will more be difficult for Mary to leave, if you're still here.

ELSPETH. ...Do you think I've burdened her, with my own grief?

MISS GILLIES. *(Sympathetically.)* ...I shouldn't have asked more of you than you could give.

>   *(**MISS GILLIES** goes.)*

>   *(**ELSPETH** looks at her case. She puts the item of clothing back. Closes the case.)*

>   *(The sound of the whistle. Eerie. Suddenly she feels cold. Unwanted. Maybe **MISS GILLIES** and **GREER** are right.)*

ELSPETH. *(To her locket.)* I'm sorry.

>   *(**ELSPETH** repacks her case. Closes it. Decided.)*

>   *(**ELSPETH** walks through the house. She is at the top of the staircase, with her suitcase.)*

>   *(House shadows enter. The lullaby. Concerned, **ELSPETH** feels something is happening.)*

>   *(As tension builds, we suddenly see the ghost of **HETTIE** appear right behind **ELSPETH**. **ELSPETH** is pushed down the stairs and lies injured at the bottom.)*

>   *(The lullaby continues.)*

>   *(**HETTIE** rips the locket from **ELSPETH**'s neck. She exits.)*

>   *(**HOUSE SHADOWS** enter with lanterns. They sing the lantern lullaby while **ELSPETH** is unconscious. It's beautiful, but haunting.)*

Scene Five

(Time has passed.)

*(**MARY** is helping **ELSPETH**. **ELSPETH** now has a dressing on her head and a crutch to help her walk.)*

*(**MARY** helps **ELSPETH** to take a few steps.)*

*(**MISS GILLIES** comes in.)*

MISS GILLIES. Oh good. You're out of bed.

ELSPETH. Thank you. Mary is a wonderful nurse.

MISS GILLIES. You must stay until you have made a full recovery, and then you can be on your way.

*(**MISS GILLIES** exits.)*

*(**MARY** and **ELSPETH** alone.)*

ELSPETH. Mary, how did you know I was going to leave?

MARY. ...

ELSPETH. You must feel that everyone has left you. Your mother, your brother, Hettie...

*(**MARY** points at **ELSPETH**.)*

And now me...

*(**MARY** makes the gesture, "why?")*

Mary, I...

(Checking no one is listening.) There are forces here that want me out. Things that I never believed in.

You feel it too?

*(**MARY** nods.)*

(Confidentially.) When I was pushed down the stairs, I could feel her, smell her presence. I believe Hettie is dead, but not dead.

> **(MARY** *nods.)*

Do you see her?

> *(Pause.)*

> **(MARY** *nods, yes.)*

And William?

> **(MARY** *nods, yes.* **MARY** *and* **ELSPETH** *look at each other. Both scared and relieved to know they're not alone.)*

Did you use anything that Hettie gave you to summon them from their graves?

> **(MARY** *shakes her head, no.)*

But what about the stone? You found that stone with Hettie's hair around it. These are for binding people together. Did she give that to you?

> **(MARY** *shakes her head, no.)*

Do you still have it?

> **(MARY** *takes it from her pocket.)*

Let me take this. I don't think it's good for you.

Mary. Mary, answer me this. Do you want the spirits to return to their graves?

> **(MARY** *thinks about it. Nods, yes.)*

All right. I'll find a way to –

> **(MARY** *grabs her arm.)*

What is it?

(**MARY** *uses her Bible. She points to a word on a page.*)

"Beware"

(**MARY** *points to a new word.*)

"of"

(**MARY** *points to a new word.*)

"The"

(**MARY** *points to a new word.*)

"Deuteronomy?"

(**MARY** *shakes her head, no. Points again.*)

Oh, "D".

(**MARY** *nods.*)

(**MARY** *now spells out a word in the same fashion.*)

"o", "l", "p", "h", "i", "n".

Beware of the Dolphin...? What does that mean?

(**MARY** *shrugs.*)

I found a dolphin pendant at Gull's Cry Cottage. It was Hettie's, wasn't it?

(**MARY** *nods.*)

Could it be that? In which case –

(**ELSPETH** *instinctively goes to touch her own locket but it's not there.*)

Oh! My locket! It's gone. Have you seen it?

Please, you must help me – [look]

*(**ELSPETH** begins frantically searching, until...)*

*(**MARY** takes from her pocket the locket.)*

(Relieved.) Oh, where was it?

*(**MARY** points upwards.)*

Upstairs. In Hettie's old room?

*(**MARY** nods, yes.)*

How did you... how did you know to look there?

*(**MARY** shrugs.)*

*(**MARY** puts it round **ELSPETH**'s neck.)*

I'm sorry I was going to leave. I thought it was for the best. The best for you.

I will sort it all out. I think I know somebody who can help.

*(Meanwhile, **AILSA** enters. She has a bucket with some items inside it.)*

*(Darkness falls as **AILSA** begins setting out some candles.)*

Scene Six

(Stack Mor. Darkness. Whistling winds. The sound of the sea.)

(ELSPETH joins AILSA.)

AILSA. You're late. We need to do this before we lose the moon.

ELSPETH. Is this where they found William's body?

AILSA. You brought all of his things?

(ELSPETH passes her the tied bag of William's things.)

And you're sure you want to banish Hettie as well?

ELSPETH. We must.

AILSA. And what have you got of hers?

ELSPETH. This stone was Hettie's. And this...

(ELSPETH produces the dolphin necklace.)

AILSA. Dolphin.

ELSPETH. Does the dolphin signify anything to you?

AILSA. No. Are you sure you want to sacrifice this? It's worth a few shillings.

ELSPETH. Yes. Get rid of the dolphin.

(AILSA creates a formation with the candles.)

(ELSPETH nervous.)

Will this really work?

AILSA. It's worked in the past. We'll send them back to their graves.

(She takes out a slate.)

This is the altar.

> *(**AILSA** takes the bag, the dolphin pendant and the stone and places the items in the bucket and puts it on the slate. She waits. **ELSPETH**, expectant.)*

We have to wait for the clouds to pass by. We need an unblinking moon.

> *(She holds **ELSPETH**'s hand.)*

Right, watch for the moon.

Now.

> *(**SPIRITS** enter.)*

> *(**AILSA** sets the bucket on fire.)*

> *(She crumbles some seaweed into the bucket.)*

> *(**AILSA** performs the banishing prayer. Dark music.)*

From the darkness of the dawn of time

I invoke all power from the shadows of the night.

*(To **ELSPETH**.)* Repeat with me.

> *(The **SPIRITS** appear. With **ELSPETH**, they repeat **AILSA**'s words, below:)*

Ateh, atch, atch

Malkuth, ve geburah,

Ve gedulah,

Le olahm, amen.

This is not the place for you.

Be gone from hence, and be at peace.

>   (**AILSA** *begins to trace out the pentagram.*)

Before me, Raphael

Behind me, Gabriel,

On my right hand, Michael

And on my left hand, Auriel

>   (**AILSA** *moves into position, the fifth place of the pentagram.*)

About me flames the pentagram.

And in the column, stands the six-rayed star.

>   (*The* **SPIRITS** *become animate as she mutters the banishing prayer/ritual/chant/dance. Sound, music, atmosphere should be all-consuming.*)

>   (**AILSA** *throws a final handful into the bucket. An explosive leap of flame. Then it's gone.*)

>   (**SPIRITS** *disappear.*)

>   (**ELSPETH** *is overawed by it all.*)

Are you all right?

ELSPETH. *(Getting her breath.)* ...Yes.

AILSA. Now we scatter some of this here where William was found. And the rest we take to the sea, where Hettie died.

>   (**ELSPETH** *and* **AILSA** *exit. Morning light grows.*)

Scene Seven

(**MARY** *and* **MISS GILLIES** *onstage. Playful.*)

MISS GILLIES. A jar? What do you need a jar for?

(**MARY** *allows* **MISS GILLIES** *to peek inside her clasped hands.*)

Hmm. I'm sure Greer will know where to lay her hands on a jar for you.

(**MARY** *runs off. Happy.*)

(**ELSPETH** *enters.*)

Something's changed, hasn't it? She seems so much lighter. You, too, Elspeth.

ELSPETH. You feel it?

MISS GILLIES. Don't you?

ELSPETH. I do. It's like the whole house has woken up from a bad dream.

MISS GILLIES. It was troubling you, before?

ELSPETH. ...I had heard Iskar has a reputation for being... haunted.

MISS GILLIES. The island does like to gossip. If it can't find something to say about the living, it will conjure up something to say about the dead.

(**ELSPETH** *plays with her locket.*)

ELSPETH. Do you...did you ever believe there was any truth in it?

MISS GILLIES. There was talk, in the house, of a ghost, but...

ELSPETH. When?

MISS GILLIES. Oh. Many years ago. But I don't believe in ghosts.

ELSPETH. Whose ghost was it supposed to be?

MISS GILLIES. A scullery maid. She fell from a window. It was most unfortunate.

ELSPETH. She fell? Or she was pushed?

MISS GILLIES. Your thoughts are too ghoulish. It was an accident. Or...

ELSPETH. She took her own life?

MISS GILLIES. No one ever knew for certain.

ELSPETH. The servant; it was Greer's mother, wasn't it?

MISS GILLIES. I see decades' old gossip still swirls around Skelthsea.

>   *(Beat.)*

ELSPETH. Did *you* ever...see anything? Or hear anything?

MISS GILLIES. You'll think me fanciful.

ELSPETH. No. There are so many noises in a grand house, like this.

MISS GILLIES. Yes.

After Greer's mother died... I sometimes imagined I could hear, at night, a whistling sound.

I wondered if I'd heard that whistle again recently. Had you...have you heard anything at all?

ELSPETH. No.

No. There's no whistle now. You don't have to worry about that anymore.

>   *(They look at each other.* **GREER** *enters.)*

GREER. Mrs Argyle is here to see Elspeth.

(**BRIDGET** *enters.*)

ELSPETH. Bridget!

BRIDGET. I came to see how you are.

MISS GILLIES. Greer, perhaps you could fetch some tea.

GREER. Of course.

MISS GILLIES. And I have business to attend to.

(**MISS GILLIES** *and* **GREER** *exit.*)

BRIDGET. I heard you'd been in an accident. I wanted to check on you.

ELSPETH. I... I fell down the stairs. But everything's all right now.

BRIDGET. If you're feeling up to it, I wanted to invite you to come round to supper. Maybe bring Mary, too. Robert asks after her all the time.

ELSPETH. That would be lovely.

BRIDGET. How are things here? I thought I saw an *actual* smile on Miss Gillies' lips?

ELSPETH. Yes. I think we've turned a corner.

BRIDGET. And Mary?

ELSPETH. She's doing much better.

BRIDGET. You should be proud. You kept persevering when others gave up. Is she speaking?

ELSPETH. It's only a matter of time. But Miss Gillies has already arranged for her to go away to the asylum.

BRIDGET. And you're sure that wouldn't be the right thing for Mary?

ELSPETH. No. She's getting better. I know she is.

Maybe you could help! Perhaps you could ask your husband to speak to Miss Gillies? If the Reverend told her that he has observed real progress in Mary and that to send her away now would only set her back, from a position of authority, Miss Gillies might listen to him.

BRIDGET. I'll ask him as soon as I get back. But if it has already been arranged...

> (**MARY** *enters. She holds a jar. Almost secretively.*)

(*Warmly.*) And there she is.

> (**BRIDGET** *holds out her arms.* **MARY** *smiles, tentatively accepts the hug.*)

What have you got there?

> (**MARY** *allows* **ELSPETH** *and* **BRIDGET** *a peek inside the jar.*)

Ah, a moth. Where did it come from?

> (**MARY** *gestures with a nod.*)

Upstairs?

> (**MARY** *nods.*)

Was it trapped?

> (**MARY** *nods.*)

Aye, easy to get trapped in a house like this.

> (**MARY** *makes a scurrying spider with her fingers.*)

A spider? Oh, it was trapped in a spider's web.

> (**MARY** *nods.*)

ELSPETH. We should release it outside.

BRIDGET. Well, then, I'd better not get in your way. I can see you have important work to do.

ELSPETH. Bridget... Thank you for coming. And you will speak to your husband, won't you?

BRIDGET. I'll do what I can.

> (**ELSPETH** *and* **BRIDGET** *smile/clasp hands.* **BRIDGET** *exits.*)

ELSPETH. You know why moths get trapped inside our houses? Moths have evolved to navigate by moonlight. The artificial light from our lamps pulls them off course. Why don't we release it beneath the moon – let her find her way.

> (*Darkness falls.*)

> (**ELSPETH** *and* **MARY** *step into a new time and space. We hear the sea.*)

You haven't seen anything of...

> (**MARY** *shakes her head, no.*)

No. Me neither. I think it worked. Whatever people of the island say about Ailsa, she has helped us. Do remember that.

Right, ready, nice and gently. And it should fly off towards the moon.

There it goes.

> (*The moth flies off.*)

It's free, Mary.

> (*The moth has gone.*)

They've gone now, haven't they? Can you feel that they've gone?

(**MARY** *nods.*)

Maybe now we can make the start I always wanted for us. You can show me the whole island. We can explore, and play!

Come on. Let's get home before it gets too cold.

(*Iskar House.*)

Do you want me to stay with you, until you're asleep?

(**MARY** *thinks about it. She's all right now. She smiles. Embraces* **ELSPETH**. *Goodnight.*)

Goodnight, Mary. Sweet dreams.

(**MARY** *smiles. Exits.*)

(*Contentedly,* **ELSPETH** *begins getting ready for bed. Then, from the silence…*)

(*The whistle.*)

(**ELSPETH** *shocked.*)

No…

(*The whistle again.*)

This can't be…

(**ELSPETH** *begins moving through the house.* **HOUSE SPIRITS** *and* **ELSPETH** *discombobulated as she tries to find where the whistle is coming from.*)

Where… where is it?

This can't be happening. We destroyed the whistle.

(*Finally,* **ELSPETH** *opens a doorway.* **GREER** *stands there with the whistle.*)

Scene Eight

(**GREER** *holding the whistle.*)

ELSPETH. So, it was you?

You've been summoning the ghosts.

GREER. You shouldn't have interfered.

ELSPETH. You're the one who interferes!

How did you get it?

GREER. You thought you could destroy it.

ELSPETH. You took it from William's things, before we...

GREER. You think you can protect yourself with your witch friend.

ELSPETH. Give me that. It should have been destroyed.

(But **GREER** *won't give it up.*)

(*Realising.*) It was you! You summoned Hettie to push me down the stairs!

GREER. Go away. You're not wanted here.

ELSPETH. You don't scare me anymore. You've tried to frighten me from the first but I know what you are. I know your wickedness. You've done your worst, and it hasn't worked on me. I'm not leaving the island. Do you understand?

GREER. You. You come to Skelthsea, thinking you're better than us all, and in no time, you're cavorting with Reid Paterson. Just as Hettie did. It's not right. It's not happening again.

ELSPETH. Oh!

You like him. Paterson.

GREER. No...

(An eerie rumble begins and builds throughout:)

ELSPETH. And he loved Hettie, not you...

So, you killed her?

GREER. No.

ELSPETH. Does Miss Gillies know what you did?

Where is she?

GREER. Miss Gillies has known me my whole life. She'd never believe you over me.

ELSPETH. Wouldn't she?

> *(**ELSPETH** about to leave. **GREER** attacks her. **ELSPETH** tries to grab the whistle from **GREER**. A tussle. The whistle is knocked to the floor. **GREER** about to hit **ELSPETH** but then sees **MARY** has entered.)*

GREER. Mary, you shouldn't be up this late. I'll take you back to your –

ELSPETH. No. I'll do it.

> *(**ELSPETH** takes **MARY** away.)*

> *(We see **GREER** notice the whistle on the floor. She pockets it. Finally, **GREER** exits. **MARY** runs to hug **ELSPETH**.)*

You told me, the other day at Gulls Cry Cottage, you told me you thought you were going to die...

I think there *is* danger here for you. And for me too. Mary, if you know more than you have told me, you must tell me now. So I can protect you.

> *(**MARY** is angry with **ELSPETH**. She turns to leave.)*

> *(**ELSPETH** grabs her.)*

I'm sorry. I said, didn't I, I promised that I wouldn't ever ask you to speak, and I meant it. I don't ever want to break a promise to you. But you have held your silence long enough. You must tell me.

> (**MARY** *pinches her lips and shakes her head. She can't say anything.*)

You can!

> (*This frightens* **MARY**.)

And you must! You must speak to me, lest both of us –

> (**MARY** *takes from her pocket a note and hands it to* **ELSPETH**.)

What is this?

> (**ELSPETH** *takes the note.*)

This isn't your handwriting.

> (**MARY** *agrees.*)

"William died because he could not keep his tongue still. If you speak of what you know, I shall still yours."

Who gave you this note?

MARY. ...

ELSPETH. Who gave it to you?

> (*Silence.*)

MARY. (*Whispering.*) ...I'm glad you didn't leave.

ELSPETH. (*Overwhelmed.*) Oh, Mary.

> (**ELSPETH** *holds* **MARY**.)

I will look after you. I promise. I promise, I promise, I promise.

Where did this note come from?

MARY. It was on my pillow.

ELSPETH. When?

MARY. After William died.

ELSPETH. And so you haven't spoken, in fear of whomever left you this note.

> (**MARY** *nods.*)

Mary, please tell me, if you can, what you know that the person who sent you this note doesn't want you to say. You can speak safely to me.

MARY. ...William. He told me that he had seen Hettie taken out to sea wrapped in the cloth.

ELSPETH. Who took her out?

MARY. He wouldn't tell me.

ELSPETH. Do you promise he didn't tell you?

MARY. He said the person had seen him and warned him not to speak.

ELSPETH. And when he was killed you protected yourself with your silence.

> (**MARY** *nods.*)

> (**ELSPETH** *holds* **MARY**.)

MARY. What will you do, Elspeth?

ELSPETH. I will think of something. And Mary, your voice is a lovely thing.

MARY. I'm afraid. I'm afraid to speak to anyone but you.

ELSPETH. Then don't. Don't speak to anyone, and don't be alone with anyone until I have worked out what is best for us.

MARY. Will you *promise* not to tell anyone that I have spoken?

ELSPETH. I promise.

Would you like to stay here tonight?

> *(**MARY** nods.)*

> *(**MARY** climbs into bed.)*

MARY. Will you hold me?

> *(**ELSPETH** lies next to her and holds her.)*

> *(Lights down.)*

> *(We hear the dripping from Gulls Cry Cottage.)*

> *(Drip.)*

BOY'S VOICE. Drip *(Repeated.)*

> *(Suddenly, **ELSPETH** sits up. We see that **ELSPETH** has had a realisation.)*

Scene Nine

(Morning light. Seagulls.)

(With great urgency, **ELSPETH** *begins knocking for* **BRIDGET**. **BRIDGET** *appears.)*

BRIDGET. Elspeth, whatever's the matter?

ELSPETH. *(Urgently.)* I've just been into Gulls Cry Cottage. You know I found Hettie's case and purse there?

BRIDGET. Yes but –

ELSPETH. There was something else. I saw it but I didn't realise what it meant. These.

> *(***ELSPETH*** holds out some knitted baby clothes.)*

Everything in Gulls Cry Cottage is old and dank, but these have been newly knitted. Hettie knitted them.

BRIDGET. I'm not sure I –

ELSPETH. She was expecting! She was with child.

> *(***BRIDGET*** takes and holds the clothes, almost as if a child is inside them.)*

BRIDGET. It was well known that Hettie and Paterson were lovers.

ELSPETH. Greer has feelings for Paterson too. Did you know that?

BRIDGET. It was gossiped about. I was never –

ELSPETH. Greer wanted rid of Hettie. She wanted the job of nannying the children and finding out that Hettie was intimate with Paterson was more than she could bear.

BRIDGET. Have you confronted Greer with this?

ELSPETH. She knows I know. She has been using a widow's whistle to raise Hettie's spirit to scare me away from Skelthsea.

BRIDGET. This sounds like Ailsa putting thoughts into your head.

ELSPETH. But I heard the whistle, felt Hettie's presence from my first night on the island. How did Greer know to raise Hettie's spirit unless she already knew Hettie was dead? She knew Hettie was dead before the body was washed up on the beach. She killed Hettie and William and now she wants to kill Mary and me.

BRIDGET. Has Mary been able to say anything yet?

ELSPETH. *(Remembering to lie.)* ...No.

BRIDGET. Then you must tell Miss Gillies.

ELSPETH. She doesn't care for Mary. She tries to pretend that she does but she's already arranged to have Mary committed to an asylum.

BRIDGET. Perhaps she'll be safer there, after all. But *you* must leave. To protect yourself, you must leave Skelthsea.

ELSPETH. I cannot leave Mary.

BRIDGET. You're a better soul than Mary could have ever wished for.

ELSPETH. I have to get her out of here, before she's killed or locked away in an asylum where her only madness is that she's frightened.

BRIDGET. You'd really take her with you?

ELSPETH. *(Realising.)* I love her, like a sister.

BRIDGET. ...But there isn't a boat now until next week.

ELSPETH. What can I do?

BRIDGET. Let me think...

There's a fisherman here who owes Robert a favour. He could take you and Mary to the mainland overnight.

ELSPETH. Could you arrange it?

BRIDGET. Yes, I think so, but are you sure this is the right thing to do?

ELSPETH. I have to. For Mary.

BRIDGET. Meet me at the North Beach at midnight. I'll go and make the arrangements. Only bring what you and Mary absolutely need. Dress warmly and be careful.

> (**BRIDGET** *exits.*)

> (*Sound of a gong chiming.*)

Scene Ten

(Nighttime. Thick mist. The sounds of a gentle sea.)

*(**ELSPETH** holds a case and a lamp; **MARY** holds an oil lamp, her case and Bobbity. They wait.)*

MARY. I've never left the island.

ELSPETH. Take something of it with you. A pebble or a shell maybe. Until you can return.

*(**MARY** picks up a shell.)*

What have you got?

*(**MARY** holds the shell up to the lantern.)*

It's a pretty one.

MARY. You've seen it before.

ELSPETH. How could I?

MARY. Ailsa said it has a pattern that looks like an "M."

ELSPETH. *(Unnerved.)* You have a way of finding things, don't you?

MARY. ...But I think it's a "W" for William.

ELSPETH. You found the stone I threw out the window; you found my locket, and now... How do you do it? How do you know where to look?

MARY. I don't know how. It's just a feeling I get that tells me where to look.

ELSPETH. Has that always been the case?

MARY. Only since William died.

ELSPETH. Is it William who guides you with these thoughts?

MARY. It feels more like Hettie.

ELSPETH. Do you get other feelings?

MARY. I knew you were going to leave. And I knew to beware of the dolphin.

ELSPETH. Well, don't worry about the dolphin – that's gone now.

MARY. Are you sure? I still get the bad feeling about it.

ELSPETH. It's destroyed. I saw it with my own eyes.

MARY. Yes, but –

ELSPETH. Shh, here's Bridget.

>　*(Purposefully,* **BRIDGET** *enters. Wrapped up for the cold night.)*

BRIDGET. Right, you two. We'll row out to the fishing boat, it's behind the point, there, as not to be seen. Then the fisherman will take you to the mainland. Are you sure you want to do this?

ELSPETH. We must.

BRIDGET. Did Greer see you leave?

ELSPETH. I don't think so.

>　*(***BRIDGET** *looks to* **MARY**.*)*

>　*(***MARY** *shakes her head, no.)*

BRIDGET. *(Gently.)* Come along.

>　*(The rowing boat and sea is created. Mist and movement.)*

>　*(They get in the boat;* **BRIDGET** *starts rowing. Splashes from the oars.)*

ELSPETH. The mist is so thick. Will we be all right?

BRIDGET. *(Good humoured.)* You're still a city girl, Elspeth. This is nothing.

ELSPETH. How will we get on the other boat?

BRIDGET. He's anchored off the water, yonder. He'll throw me a line and you and Mary will have to ladder it up the side.

ELSPETH. Will you be safe rowing back alone? There's another storm coming in.

BRIDGET. Ah, *The Dolphin*, she's seen much worse. *(Patting the boat affectionately.)*

> *(**ELSPETH** and **MARY** both hit with horror. They are in 'The Dolphin'. Music and lights should indicate their sudden terror.)*

ELSPETH. The Dolphin?

BRIDGET. Aye, that's what my father named her.

What's wrong?

> *(**ELSPETH** reevaluates **BRIDGET**.)*

ELSPETH. How...how far to the other boat?

> *(No answer. **BRIDGET** just keeps rowing.)*

Bridget. How far...

> *(A stony look from **BRIDGET**.)*

There is no other boat, is there?

> *(Beat.)*

BRIDGET. I could have put up with the affair. But she was going to give Robert what he most wanted.

ELSPETH. Bridget?

BRIDGET. You were right, Elspeth. Hettie was expecting a child. Oh, she'd been intimate with Paterson at one

time or another, but it was Robert who lost his heart
to her and gave her what I wanted with all of *my* heart.

ELSPETH. So, you killed her? Hettie was carrying Robert's
child so you –

BRIDGET. She was evil. And she found a kindred spirit in
William.

MARY. They were not evil! She's lying, Elspeth. Hettie was
good and so was William.

BRIDGET. William used to sacrifice animals up on Stack
Mor. Everyone talked about it.

MARY. William never hurt animals; he loved them.

ELSPETH. *You* spread the rumours of William's evil.

BRIDGET. *(Sinister.)* You know I'm not one to *gossip*.

ELSPETH. And it was you who fabricated word of Hettie's
wickedness. Why?

BRIDGET. If I made it so that Hettie was wicked, Robert
would leave her. A man of God. But still he continued
to love her.

ELSPETH. And William? He saw you. *(To* **MARY**.*)* Didn't
he? *(To* **BRIDGET**.*)* He saw you rowing Hettie's body out
to sea.

BRIDGET. Inquisitive children always find trouble for
themselves. He saw me row Hettie's body out to sea. I
threatened him into secrecy but I knew he would tell
his twin *(Scowling at* **MARY**.*)* So, I started a rumour,
that William was inflicted with the same darkness as
Hettie. Who would question God for punishing him for
his satanic rituals up on Stack Mor? And now you both
have to face the same fate.

ELSPETH. Bridget. We can work this out. We're friends,
aren't we? I can help you, Bridget. Mary and I are the
only ones who know. We can keep it between us. Why
don't we go back to land and –

BRIDGET. It's too late for that.

ELSPETH. Please, turn the boat around –

BRIDGET. No. This is the only way.

> (**ELSPETH** *tries to fight* **BRIDGET** *for the oars.* **MARY** *tries to help* **ELSPETH** *but* **BRIDGET** *knocks* **ELSPETH** *out with an oar.* **ELSPETH** *is unconscious in the boat.*)

> (**BRIDGET** *now turns on* **MARY**. *She approaches* **MARY** *who backs away, but there's only so far she can go.*)

Inquisitive children *always* find trouble for themselves.

> (**BRIDGET** *is just about to push* **MARY** *overboard.*)

> (*We hear from the distance the whistle being blown.*)

> (*As* **BRIDGET** *turns back to* **MARY**, **HETTIE** *appears behind her. A look of vengeance.* **BRIDGET** *terrified. But it's too late to react.*)

> (*Blackout.*)

> (*The Lullaby is sung.*)

Scene Eleven

> *(Iskar House.* **ELSPETH** *and* **MARY** *sit with blankets wrapped round them.)*

GREER. Here, drink this.

ELSPETH. I can't help but think of her little body floating away on the waves. After everything Mary has been through.

GREER. Come on. Take a sip. It'll warm you.

ELSPETH. You blew the whistle to bring Hettie back. You knew she would help us.

> (**ELSPETH** *goes to put her hand on* **GREER***'s.)*

Thank y–

> *(***GREER** *pulls away.)*

But how did you know, Greer? How did you know we'd be there?

> *(***GREER** *doesn't know how to explain.)*

GREER. Bridget. She spoke to me this afternoon.

ELSPETH. Bridget told you. Were you helping her?

GREER. I didn't want to. She...

(Eventually.) A long time ago I took a confession to Robert Argyle at the church. I didn't know that Bridget Argyle was listening.

ELSPETH. What had you done?

GREER. *(Suddenly angry.)* It was their fault. Evangeline and Violet Gillies. They were so cruel to their scullery maid – my mother. Making fun of her, because she wasn't like other people. In her mind. In her manner. Young girls making an adult woman weep in her bed. Until she could bear it no longer.

ELSPETH. You think your mother jumped from the window?

GREER. I believe so.

ELSPETH. So, what did you do to them?

GREER. The "inseparable" sisters shared a room. One night, I went in and I pushed their candle too close to the curtains.

ELSPETH. The fire…

GREER. I just meant to scare them but –

ELSPETH. It was because of you the house burnt down.

GREER. Miss Gillies thought it was Evangeline's fault. She blamed her sister for the fire, for her face. If she found out it was me, that I had caused her scars, she'd have banished me from the only home I ever knew.

ELSPETH. And so Bridget was able to manipulate you…

GREER. When Bridget found out about her husband and Hettie, she forced me to create pagan stone formations and leave bones of sacrificed animals up on Stack Mor, where Hettie and William were often seen.

ELSPETH. And the whistle? Where did you get such a thing?

GREER. My grandmother, she had gifts. She told me what it was for and that I could use it, if I ever needed. I put it with the items I'd put in William's wing.

ELSPETH. But why have you been using it to call Hettie all this time?

(*Accusingly.*) You knew Hettie wanted to harm me and you called and called her night after night! It was Hettie who pushed me down the stairs.

GREER. I called Hettie to scare you, it's true. But I had no control over what she did. And she knew better than I. Can't you see? She pushed you down the stairs to stop you leaving. To keep you here with Mary!

ELSPETH. And tonight you blew the whistle to bring Hettie back. You knew she would help us.

GREER. Hettie loved those children.

ELSPETH. So do you.

GREER. Yes.

(**ELSPETH** *warming to* **GREER**.)

ELSPETH. Did you see what I saw? Hettie...

GREER. I'm sure of it. She pushed Bridget into the sea, so she could never return, never harm anyone again.

I can't take back what I did, Elspeth. But at least you understand it now.

(**MARY** *appears.*)

ELSPETH. Mary!

MARY. I miss Bobbity.

ELSPETH. I'm so sorry. Think of her as swimming to a new adventure.

(**GREER** *turns to leave.*)

Greer.

GREER. Yes?

ELSPETH. Thank you.

GREER. You're welcome, miss.

(**GREER** *exits.*)

(**ELSPETH** *sees the whistle.*)

ELSPETH. The whistle...

MARY. I know what you're thinking...

ELSPETH. What if I *could* call Clara back?

MARY. *(Shaking her head, no.)* They don't like to be called from their rest. William, Hettie, when they were here, I could feel it. Their unhappiness.

ELSPETH. Just once. Just to see her...

> *(**ELSPETH** lifts the whistle to her lips. **MARY** puts her hand on the whistle.)*

MARY. No! You can't, Elspeth. Clara's at rest. It's not she who needs you.

> *(**ELSPETH** realises that it is **MARY** who needs her now.)*

You saved me.

ELSPETH. No. Hettie, she saved us both.

She loved you, dearly. I can tell.

MARY. And I loved her. But I love you like a sister.

ELSPETH. I came here to help you but I wonder if it is you who has helped me.

> *(**ELSPETH** holds her.)*

What should we do with this? [The whistle]

MARY. You don't need it. If we want to see those we've lost, we just have to close our eyes.

> *(**ELSPETH** closes her eyes.)*

What do you see?

ELSPETH. ...Clara. Not in the photograph but how we used to be. Walking through the bustle of the Edinburgh streets. Without a care, so long as we had each other.

What do you see?

> *(**MARY** closes her eyes.)*

MARY. I can see them. William and Hettie. Down on the beach.

They're growing fainter...becoming part of the grass, and the wind...the sea...

ELSPETH. *(Still with eyes closed.)* And what do we do now?

MARY. *(Still with eyes closed.)* We let them go.

(They hold hands.)

(Music.)

The End

Milton Keynes UK
Ingram Content Group UK Ltd.
UKHW021846051224
452124UK00011B/318